The Logit model

AN INTRODUCTION

The Logit model

FOR ECONOMISTS

J.S. CRAMER
University of Amsterdam

Edward Arnold
A division of Hodder & Stoughton
LONDON NEW YORK MELBOURNE AUCKLAND

First published in Great Britain 1991

Distributed in the USA by Routledge, Chapman and Hall Inc.
29 West 35th Street, New York, NY 10001

British Library Cataloguing in Publication Data
Cramer, J. S.
The LOGIT model : an introduction for economists.
1. Econometrics. Regression analysis
I. Title
330.072

ISBN 0-340-54111-3

Typeset in Times by MS Filmsetting Limited, Frome, Somerset
Printed and bound in Great Britain for Edward Arnold,
a division of Hodder and Stoughton Limited,
Mill Road, Dunton Green, Sevenoaks, Kent TN13 2YA
by Biddles Limited, Guildford and King's Lynn

Preface

While probability models are nowadays used as a matter of course to model discrete choice in economic studies, their theoretical background and their estimation are often regarded as a matter of advanced econometrics. The aim of this introductory monograph is to render one model of this type, namely the logit model, accessible to all, and to put it on the same footing as standard linear regression. The reader is assumed to be familiar with that model, and with the elements of estimation theory and matrix algebra that go with it.

By the nature of this undertaking the present text contains very little that is novel. I have freely drawn on the existing literature, and I can only hope that the reader will follow up the references and continue her or his instruction at first hand from the original sources.

I am indebted to Jörgen Wit for drawing the figures. All the examples have been worked with Doornik's excellent LOGITJD programme.

J. S. Cramer
Amsterdam, February 1990

Contents

List of Tables

List of Figures

1
Introduction

1.1 The role of the logit model

By its origins, and by its current use in economic analysis, the logit model is the natural complement of the regression model in case the regressand is not a continuous variable but a state which may or may not obtain, or a category in a given classification. When such variables occur among the regressors of a regression equation, they can be dealt with by the introduction of (0,1) dummy variables; but when the dependent variable belongs to this type, the regression model breaks down. In this case of **qualitative dependent variables** the logit model provides a ready alternative. At first sight it is quite different from the familiar linear regression model, and slightly frightening by its apparent complexity; yet the two models have much in common.

First, both models belong to the realm of a causal relations, as opposed to statistical association; there is a clear *a priori* asymmetry between the independent variables or regressors, and the dependent variable or regressand. Both models have originally been designed for the analysis of experimental data, or at least for data where the direction of causation is beyond doubt. In interpreting empirical applications it is often helpful to bear these origins in mind.

Within this causal context, the simple linear regression model offers a crude but almost universal framework for empirical analysis. Admittedly it is often only a simplified approximation to something else that would presumably be something better; but it does serve, within its limitations, for empirical screening of the evidence. The logit model can be used in quite the same way for explanatory models of categorical phenomena.

There are of course also differences. Quite unlike regression, the logit model permits of a specific economic interpretation in terms of utility maximisation in situations of discrete choice. Some adherents of this view may even feel offended by the presentation of the model as a merely convenient empirical device. And there is a subtle distinction in that regression needs a disturbance term which is stuck on to the systematic part as a necessary nuisance, while in the logit model (as in all probability models) the random character of the dependent variable follows naturally from the initial specification.

Finally, like the regression model, the logit model permits of extensions and of quite sophisticated variants, and there exist a number of related alternatives. I shall touch upon some of these themes in the later chapters, but in the main I shall be concerned with the logit model in its simpler form as a convenient vehicle for the econometric analysis of the determination of categorical variables.

1.2 Plan of the book

The book consists of this chapter and four others. Chapters 2 and 3 are straightforward presentations of the classical bivariate and multinomial logit models, here denoted as the standard models. Chapter 2 develops the simple bivariate model, and Chapter 3 deals with the standard multinomial generalisation. We set out the models, deal briefly with their properties, derive the formulae for maximum likelihood estimation and give an example. Chapter 4 sets out some further developments of the model specification within the logit framework. Chapter 5 finally deals with the use of accepted and estimated logit models for prediction and simulation, and moreover addresses the vexed question of measures of goodness of fit. While we still take the logit model as our example, most of this chapter applies to the wider class of probability models.

Inevitably, we must at times introduce elements that are only at a later stage used to their full extent. The powerful utility maximisation background of the multinomial model is for instance set out in Chapter 3, but not deployed to its full advantage until Chapter 4. There are other examples of anticipation.

Since this is after all a slim book, designed for newcomers to the subject, we expect the reader to skim through the entire text, and then to return at leisure to the bits she or he can use, or—still better—to continue at once with further reading. For a general introduction we recommend such varied texts as the classical book by Finney (1971), the excellent works of Amemiya (the survey article of 1981 or Chapter 9 of the book of 1985), the discrete choice textbook of Lerman and Ben-Akiva (1976) and Maddala's wide ranging survey (1983). And then the articles in learned journals that are quoted are there to be read.

Most of the present material is fairly elementary and apart from minor parts of Chapter 5 nothing is novel. I hope the reader will find his way to the current literature for more advanced contributions to the subject.

1.3 Notation

I have aimed at a consistent use of various scripts and fonts while respecting established usage, but the resulting notation is not altogether uniform. It is also often incomplete in the sense that it can only be understood in the context in which it is used. A full classification with a distinct notation for each type of expression and variable is so cumbersome that it would hinder understanding: as in all writing, completeness does not ensure clarity. I must therefore put my trust in the good sense of the reader. My main misgiving is that I found no room for a separate typographical distinction between random variables and their realisation; in the end the distinction of boldface type was awarded to vectors and matrices as opposed to scalars.

The first broad distinction is that, as a rule, the Greek alphabet is used for unknown parameters and for other unobservables, such as disturbances, and

Latin letters for everything else. But Greek letters are also occasionally employed for specific functions, like the Normal distribution function.

In either alphabet there is a distinction between scalars and vectors or matrices. Scalars are usually designated by capital letters, without further distinction, but vectors and matrices are set in boldface, with lower-case letters for (column) vectors and capitals for matrices. I use a superscript T for transposition, the dash being exclusively reserved for differentiation.

The differentiation of vector functions of a scalar and of scalar functions of a vector habitually causes notational problems. In an expression like

$$\mathbf{y} = \mathbf{f}(X)$$

$\mathbf{y}$ is a column vector with elements that are functions of a scalar X. Differentiation will yield $\mathbf{f}'$, which is again a column vector. But in

$$Y = f(\mathbf{x})$$

the scalar Y is a function of several arguments that have been arranged in the column vector $\mathbf{x}$. Differentiation in respect of (the elements of) $\mathbf{x}$ will yield a number of partial derivatives, which we arrange, by convention, in a **row** vector $\mathbf{f}'$. By the same logic, if $\mathbf{y}$ is an $r \times 1$ vector and $\mathbf{x}$ a $s \times 1$ vector, and

$$\mathbf{y} = \mathbf{f}(\mathbf{x})$$

$\mathbf{f}'$ is an $r \times s$ matrix of partial derivatives, and in naming it we should use a capital letter.

We use the standard terms of estimation theory and statistics, such as the expectation operator E, the variance of a scalar var and the variance–covariance matrix $\mathbf{V}$, applying them directly to the random variable to which they refer, as in EZ, var Z, and $\mathbf{Vz}$. The arguments on which these (and other) expressions depend are indicated in parentheses. Thus

$$\mathbf{Vz}(\boldsymbol{\theta})$$

indicates that the variance matrix of $\mathbf{z}$ is a function of the parameter vector $\boldsymbol{\theta}$, while

$$\mathbf{V}\hat{\boldsymbol{\theta}}$$

is the variance matrix of $\hat{\theta}$. This is an estimate of θ, as indicated by the circumflex above it. Again,

$$\hat{\mathbf{V}}\mathbf{z} = \mathbf{Vz}(\hat{\theta})$$

indicates how an estimated variance matrix is obtained.

Probabilities abound. We write

$$\Pr(Y = 1)$$

for the probability of an event, described within brackets, but

$$P(X)$$

for a probability that is a function of X. The vector $\mathbf{p}$ consists of a number of probabilities that invariably sum to one.

Cross references to sections are always given in full. All equations are numbered by chapter. Equations within the same chapter are referred to by their serial number, and equations in other chapters by double numbers.

2

The Bivariate Model

2.1 The logit model for a single attribute

Together with other probability models for qualitative dependent variables, the logit model has its origins in the analysis of biological experiments. If samples of insects are exposed to an insecticide at various levels of concentration, the proportion killed varies with the dosage. For a single animal this is an experiment with a determinate, continuously variable stimulus and an uncertain or random discrete response, viz. survival or death. The same scheme applies to patients who are given a treatment at varying intensity, and who do or do not recover, or to consumer households at different levels of income who respond to this incentive by owning or not owning a car or some other durable good. This last case is an example of discrete choice in consumer behaviour. The class of phenomena and models we have thus loosely defined is variously denoted in the biological literature as **quantal variables** or as **stimulus and response models**, in econometrics as **qualitative** or **limited dependent variables**, and in psychology and economics as **discrete choice**.

We examine the car ownership example more closely. The relation of car ownership to income can be observed in a sample survey among households. The independent variable is household income, which is continuous, and the dependent variable is ownership status, which is an attribute, or a qualitative or discrete variable. For a single attribute, like car ownership, this dependent variable Y is a scalar which can take only two values, conventionally assigned the values 0 and 1, and defined as

$$Y_i = 1 \text{ if household } i \text{ owns a car} \tag{1a}$$

$$Y_i = 0 \text{ otherwise} \tag{1b}$$

When these values are plotted against income X_i for a sample of households we obtain the scatter diagram of Fig. 2.1. A regression line could be fitted to these data by the usual technique, but the underlying model that makes sense of this exercise does not apply.* One may of course even in this case still **define** a linear relationship, and make it hold identically by the introduction of an additive disturbance ε_i, as in

$$Y_i = \alpha + \beta X_i + \varepsilon_i \tag{2}$$

* There is no short-cut formula for the linear regression of Y on X. If X were regressed on Y, however, the regression line would pass through the mean incomes of car owners and of non car owners.

In order to restrict the Y_i to the observed values 0 and 1, however, complex properties must be attributed to the disturbance ε_i; it cannot have the simple properties that are the main appeal of the regression model. The observed points can not possibly have been generated by a general function

$$Y = \alpha + \beta X + \varepsilon \tag{3}$$

with any reasonable specification of the random ε.

Instead, the natural approach to the data of Fig. 2.1 is to regard Y_i as a discrete random variable, and to make the probability of $Y_i = 1$, not the value of Y_i itself, a suitable function of the regressor X. This leads to a **probability model** which specifies the probability of a certain response as a function of the stimulus, as in

$$P_i = \Pr(Y_i = 1) = P(X_i, \boldsymbol{\theta}) \tag{4a}$$

$$Q_i = \Pr(Y_i = 0) = 1 - P(X_i, \boldsymbol{\theta}) = Q(X_i, \boldsymbol{\theta}) \tag{4b}$$

We recall that, as a matter of notation, we use $\Pr(A)$ for the probability of the event A, $P(.)$ for a probability as a function of certain arguments, and P as a shorthand notation for either; $Q(.)$ and Q are the complements of $P(.)$ and P. In (4), $P(.)$ is a function of X_i, and the vector $\boldsymbol{\theta}$ of parameters that govern its behaviour has been added for the sake of completeness. In the sequel we shall often turn to a simpler and more careless notation.

The regression equation (2) may be briefly revived by specifying

$$P(X) = \alpha + \beta X \tag{5}$$

which is the **linear probability model**. It leads to (2), and hence to the estimation of α and β by linear regression methods, with suitable embellishments like a correction for heteroscedasticity; see Goldberger (1964, p. 250), or, for a fuller

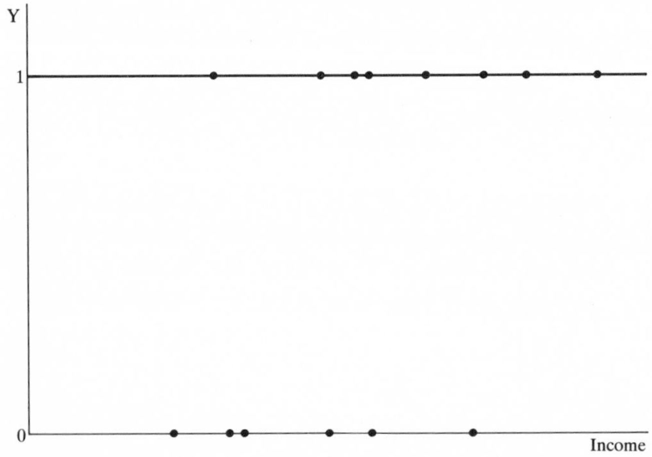

Fig. 2.1 Car ownership as a function of income in a sample of households.

treatment and a comparison with statistical discrimination, Ladd (1966). But such technical improvements do not remove the principal objection, which is that the linear specification is not constrained to the limited range from 0 to 1 which is imposed on probabilities. If we wish the probability to vary monotonically with X and yet remain within these bounds, we must look for a **sigmoid** or S-shaped curve which flattens out at either end so as to respect these natural limits. There are of course a great many functions that meet this requirement; one of these is the **logistic function**, that is

$$P(X) = \exp(\alpha + \beta X)/(1 + \exp(\alpha + \beta X)) \quad (6a)$$

$$Q(X) = 1 - P(X) = 1/(1 + \exp(\alpha + \beta X)) \quad (6b)$$

Throughout the present chapter we denote this particular probability function $P(.)$ as Pl (with **l** for **logit** or **logistic**). This is defined as

$$Pl(Z) = \exp Z/(1 + \exp Z) \quad (7)$$

so that (6a) can be written as

$$P(X) = Pl(\alpha + \beta X) \quad (8)$$

There is no direct intuitive justification for the use of this particular function. We shall in due course explain its origins, list its properties and illustrate its merits. Note already, however, that

$$1 - Pl(Z) = Pl(-Z) \quad (9)$$

so that (6) yields the pair

$$P(X) = Pl(\alpha + \beta X) \quad (10a)$$

$$Q(X) = Pl(-\alpha - \beta X) \quad (10b)$$

Also note that the inverse transformation of $Pl(Z)$ is quite simple. This is the **log odds ratio** $R(Z)$

$$R(Z) = \log(P(Z)/(1 - P(Z))) \quad (11)$$

Clearly we have $R(Z) = Z$ if $P(Z) = Pl(Z)$, and if (8) obtains

$$R(X) = \alpha + \beta X \quad (12)$$

The behaviour of the logistic function is fairly simple. The derivative in respect of X is

$$\begin{aligned} Pl'(\alpha + \beta X) &= Pl(\alpha + \beta X)(1 - Pl(\alpha + \beta X))\beta \quad (13) \\ &= P(X)Q(X)\beta \end{aligned}$$

which has the same sign as β. If β is positive, $Pl(\alpha + \beta X)$ increases monotonically from zero to one as X ranges over the entire real line, which is precisely what we require from a probability function in the examples under review. The logistic function follows the sigmoid curve shown in Fig. 2.2, which has a point of

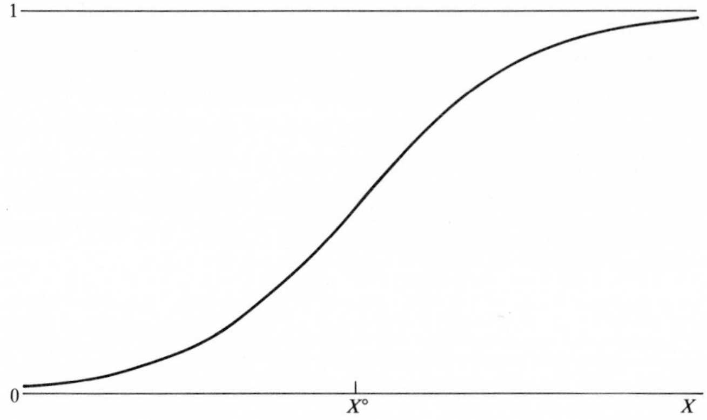

Fig. 2.2 The logistic curve $Pl(\alpha + \beta x)$.

inflexion at $Pl(0) = 0.5$, that is at $X°$ which satisfies $\alpha + \beta X° = 0$, or $X° = -\alpha/\beta$. It follows from (9) that it is symmetric around this midpoint, in the sense that the same curve is obtained if we reverse the direction of the X-axis and then turn the diagram upside down. The original curve and this mirror image cross at the midpoint $X°$ with $Pl(0) = 0.5$. The **slope** of the curve is governed by β, and at the point of inflexion it equals $\beta/4$. For a given slope, the **position** of the curve is of course determined by the parameter α.

Several other summary characteristics can be derived from the two parameters. Insecticides and similar products are often graded by the midpoint concentration level $X° = -\alpha/\beta$, known as the **50% effective dosage**, or **ED50**. In economic analyses the main interest is however in effects, not levels, and these effects are generally expressed in **elasticities** of the form

$$\mathrm{dlog}\, W/\mathrm{dlog}\, V$$

for any pair of causally related variables W and V. The popular interpretation is that this elasticity represents 'the percentage change in W upon a one percent change in V', and the major reason why it is preferred to the corresponding derivative is that it is invariant to the arbitrary choice of units of measurements of both variables. In the present case, however, the dependent variable is a probability, and its scale is not arbitrary, for it ranges from 0 to 1. We therefore recommend the use of **quasi-elasticities**, defined as

$$\eta = \mathrm{d}P(X)/\mathrm{dlog}\, X \qquad (14)$$

and given in the present instance by

$$\eta(X) = Pl(\alpha + \beta X)(1 - Pl(\alpha + \beta X))\beta X \qquad (15)$$

This quasi-elasticity indicates the percentage point change of the probability upon a one percent increase of X. Like the derivative (and the elasticity) its value varies with X, and we shall usually evaluate it at the sample mean or some other convenient point.* As P and Q sum to one, their derivatives sum to zero, and so do the quasi-elasticities; we have

$$dQ(X)/d\log X = -dP(X)/d\log X \qquad (16)$$

Genuine elasticities do not have this attractive property.

Several simple and self-evident extensions of the model come to mind. First, (6a) implies that car ownership becomes a near certainty at very high income levels. For cars this is an acceptable approximation, but for other durable goods like sports equipment or musical instruments we should set a (positive) upper limit ω of less than 1. This is the **saturation level** of those durable goods, and we then have the model

$$P(X) = \omega Pl(\alpha + \beta X) \qquad (17)$$

In the controlled laboratory conditions of bio-assay, the concentration of the insecticide is the only observable cause of death, all other conditions being kept constant as far as is feasible. But car ownership is affected by many other household characteristics apart from income, and in the design of household surveys their variation can not be prevented. In a random sample from the population we must therefore allow for several obvious additional determinants of car ownership, like family size, age of head of household, region and degree of urbanisation. The logit model easily accommodates such additional regressor variables, as in

$$P(X) = Pl(\mathbf{x}^T\boldsymbol{\beta}) \qquad (18)$$

where $\mathbf{x}$ and $\boldsymbol{\beta}$ are vectors, so that $\mathbf{x}^T\boldsymbol{\beta}$ stands for a linear combination like

$$\mathbf{x}^T\boldsymbol{\beta} = \beta_0 + \beta_1 X_1 + \beta_2 X_2 + \cdots$$

Any linear function of relevant regressor variables can thus be inserted in the logistic function; its argument may indeed be treated exactly like a regression equation. It should as a rule include a dummy constant '1' with the intercept parameter α or β_0 as its coefficient. Just as in a regression function the other regressor variables may be transformed, e.g. by taking logarithms or by adding squares, and qualitative regressors may be represented by (0,1) dummy variables.†

2.2 Justification of the model

We have already said that the logit model has no immediate intuitive appeal. It can however be justified in several ways: as a simple approximation to other probability models, by the consideration of random processes, or by its

* Note that the probability at the sample mean $\bar{X}$, $Pl(\alpha + \beta\bar{X})$, is not in general exactly equal to the sample mean of Y, that is the sample frequency of $Y = 1$, because of the nonlinearity of $Pl(.)$.

† There are no objections of principle or of technique to the use of nonlinear expressions as argument of the logistic function, but this seldom adds anything of substance to the analysis.

derivation from models of individual behaviour. The last approach offers the major advantage of a ready interpretation of the parameters; in economic applications it even permits an interpretation in utility terms. We review these arguments for the case of a single regressor variable X, but they are equally valid with several independent variables.

We begin with the approximation argument, which is quite similar to viewing the linear regression equation as an approximation to some more complex analytical relation between the regressors and the regressand.* The logit model can be regarded in the same light as an approximation to any other probability model, provided the **log odds ratio** (11) is taken as the starting point of the analysis. This ratio has been defined for any $P(X)$ as

$$R(X) = \log(P(X)/(1 - P(X)))$$

A Taylor series expansion around X^* yields

$$\begin{aligned} R(X) &= R(X^*) + R'(X^*)(X - X^*) + \text{remainder} \\ &= (R(X^*) - R'(X^*)X^*) + R'(X^*)X + \text{remainder} \end{aligned} \tag{19}$$

The first term is a constant, the second is linear in X, and the remainder represents terms in the higher-order derivatives. If $P(X)$ is the logistic function $Pl(\alpha + \beta X)$, the linear function holds exactly, and the remainder is zero, as already noted in (12). For other probability functions, the linear part constitutes an approximation. Its quality depends on the form of $P(X)$, and in particular on its higher derivatives; but these do not easily lend themselves to further discussion. This rationale of the logistic specification may appear somewhat contrived, yet it is not inferior to the common justification of a linear regression equation when this is fully spelled out.

A second argument leading to the logit model is to consider a random process in which individuals alternate between two states, such as sickness and health, employment and unemployment. The durations of spells of either state are nonnegative random variables; if they are affected by the regressor X, various models will lead to an **expected duration** of the intervals spent in states 0 and 1 of the form

$$\exp(\alpha_0 + \beta_0 X) \tag{20a}$$

$$\exp(\alpha_1 + \beta_1 X) \tag{20b}$$

which avoids negative values. Under quite general conditions the probability of finding an individual drawn at random in state 1 is then

$$P(X) = \exp(\alpha_1 + \beta_1 X)/(\exp(\alpha_0 + \beta_0 X) + \exp(\alpha_1 + \beta_1 X)) \tag{21}$$

see Ross (1977, Ch. 5). Since the numerator and the denominator can be multiplied by exp $(\delta + \zeta X)$ without affecting $P(X)$, the parameters are not

* See Cramer (1969, p. 79–83) for a closer examination of this argument.

identified; we therefore **normalise** them by putting

$$\alpha = \alpha_1 - \alpha_0, \qquad \beta = \beta_1 - \beta_0 \tag{22}$$

or, what comes to the same thing,

$$\alpha_0 = 0, \quad \beta_0 = 0, \qquad \alpha_1 = \alpha, \quad \beta_1 = \beta \tag{23}$$

Upon substitution in (21) this yields the logit model (6).

The logit model, and indeed all probability models, may also be derived from a model of underlying individual behaviour involving random elements. Such models introduce one or more unobservable or **latent** continuous variables which depend on the stimulus and trigger the discrete response. There are several variants of this approach which yield much the same result.

The first example is the **threshold** model, which provides the classical interpretation of the insecticide example. The discrete character of the dependent variable is sometimes determined by its nature, but more often imposed by the purpose of the analysis. The primary effect of an insecticide is to make insects ill in varying degree, and this might in principle be measured on a continuous scale; but it is much simpler, and sufficient for the purpose at hand, to observe merely whether the pests die or survive. Similarly we might measure a household's desire for a car of its own on a continuous scale, with ownership depending on the passage of a certain critical level; but this raises all sorts of conceptual questions, and it would certainly be much harder to observe than actual ownership, which is the standard object of analysis.

Such ideas are the basis of the threshold model. Assume a continuous (unobservable) **impact** X^* which is a linear function of the stimulus X with a random disturbance, as in a regression equation,

$$X^* = \alpha_1 + \beta_1 X + \varepsilon_1 \tag{24}$$

and a **threshold** X° given similarly by

$$X^\circ = \alpha_2 + \beta_2 X + \varepsilon_2 \tag{25}$$

Assume also that

$$Y = 1 \text{ if } X^* > X^\circ \tag{26a}$$

$$Y = 0 \text{ otherwise} \tag{26b}$$

This gives

$$\begin{aligned} P(X) &= \Pr(Y = 1) = \Pr(X^\circ < X^*) \\ &= \Pr((\varepsilon_2 - \varepsilon_1) < (\alpha_1 - \alpha_2) + \beta_1 - \beta_2)X) \end{aligned} \tag{27}$$

or

$$\begin{aligned} P(X) &= F^*((\alpha_1 - \alpha_2) + (\beta_1 - \beta_2)X) \\ &= F((\alpha - \mu)/\sigma + (\beta/\sigma)X) \end{aligned} \tag{28a}$$

with

$$\begin{aligned} \alpha &= \alpha_1 - \alpha_2, \qquad \beta = \beta_1 - \beta_2 \\ \mu &= \mu_1 - \mu_2, \qquad \sigma^2 = \sigma_1^2 + \sigma_2^2 \end{aligned} \tag{28b}$$

μ_1, μ_2 and σ_1^2, σ_2^2 of course denote the means and variances of the two disturbances, which are assumed independent. $F^*(.)$ is the distribution function of $\varepsilon = \varepsilon_2 - \varepsilon_1$, and $F(.)$ is the distribution function of the corresponding standardised variate with zero mean and unit variance. We shall see in the next section that with a suitable specification of the distribution of ε $F^*(.)$ turns into the logistic function.

Clearly this general formulation is heavily overparametrised; several restrictions are in order to achieve identification. One way is to put

$$\begin{aligned} \alpha_1 &= 0, \qquad \beta_1 = 1, \qquad \varepsilon_1 = 0, \\ \alpha_2 &= 0, \qquad \beta_2 = 0 \end{aligned} \tag{29}$$

The result is that the observed stimulus X itself is directly compared to a random threshold, which represents the individual resistance or **tolerance level** of insects or households. The slope of the distribution function $F^*(.)$ now equals $1/\sigma_2$, and thus reflects the variability of the individual tolerance levels, or the heterogeneity of the population under review.

A different simplification is to put

$$\mu_1 = 0, \qquad \beta_2 = 0, \qquad \varepsilon_2 = 0 \tag{30}$$

so that a latent disease or desire with a random component is compared to a common nonrandom threshold α_2; in this case only the ratios $(\alpha_1 - \alpha_2)/\sigma_1$ and β_1/σ_1 are identified.

By (26) the **response function** for any single experiment looks like the step function of Fig. 2.3. One interpretation of the transition to a probability function

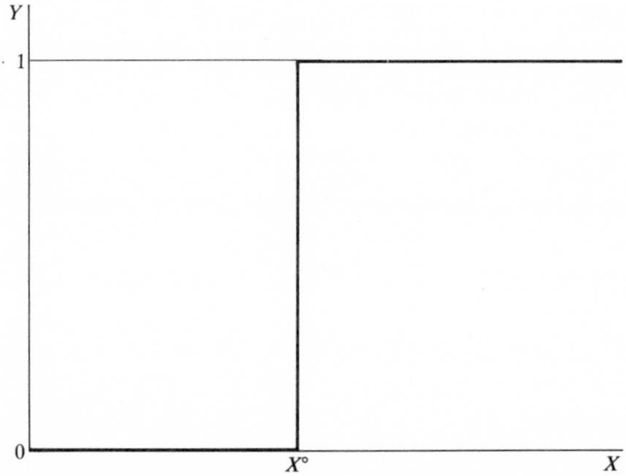

Fig. 2.3 An individual response function of the model of eq. (26).

is that the position of the critical level, or of the threshold, is a random variable for each individual insect or household, determined as it were each time the question arises by a random drawing from the appropriate distribution. But we may equally well assume that the threshold is a determinate characteristic of the individual, which shows some dispersion in the population under review. The probability model then arises because each individual constitutes a random drawing from this population. In the absence of repeated measurements on the same individual we have no means of discriminating between these two interpretations, and the choice between them is a matter of taste.

In the **utility** or **discrete choice** model the individual or the household is supposed to attach separate random utilities to the two possible states $Y = 1$ and $Y = 0$. These utilities vary with the conditions represented by the regressor variables, as in

$$U_1 = \alpha_1 + \beta_1 X + \varepsilon_1 \tag{31a}$$

$$U_0 = \alpha_2 + \beta_2 X + \varepsilon_2 \tag{31b}$$

Utility maximisation implies that the state with the higher utility obtains, that is

$$P(X) = \Pr(Y = 1) = \Pr(U_0 < U_1) \tag{32}$$

or, with the same derivation as above,

$$P(X) = F((\alpha_1 - \alpha_2)/\sigma + ((\beta_1 - \beta_2)/\sigma)X) \tag{33}$$

where we have already made the standard assumption $\mu_1, \mu_2 = 0$. The logistic function follows again upon an appropriate specification of the distribution of $\varepsilon_2 - \varepsilon_1$. The parameters α reflect the utility levels attached to each alternative, and the β the effect of the regressor on this utility. Note that we can only identify utility differentials, not levels; this is in keeping with the view that utility measures at best permit the ordering of alternatives.

These behavioural models have a distinct romantic flavour, enhanced by certain further elaborations. When log X gives better results than X in terms of fit, as is often the case, and certainly standard practice in the original field of bio-assay, this is sometimes attributed to the **law of proportionate effect** or **Weber–Fechner law**, which says that the physiological impact of a stimulus is an exponential function of its physical strength.* We shall give a fuller treatment of the utility model in Section 3.3. Whatever one may think of these theories, it must be admitted that they do provide a ready interpretation of estimated parameter values.

All these behavioural models presuppose a causal relation between the original stimulus X, some intermediate latent variable like the impact or utility, and the ultimate effect Y. In the earlier 'approximation' and 'alternating states' arguments, X moreover clearly stands for external determinants. There is always a definite asymmetry between X and Y in the sense that X is the cause and Y the

* This law was empirically established in the middle of the nineteenth century by such experiments as asking subjects to select the heavier of two weights. The standard reference is Fechner (1860).

(uncertain) effect, without any feedback, so that the value of X is not affected by the actual outcome Y. In Section 2.4 we use this basic assumption to justify the treatment of X in estimation.

The idea of a joint distribution of Y and X without a clear causal link from the one to the other is thus alien to the models under review, and it will not be followed up in this book. This applies also to the analysis of the joint distribution of several regressors $X_1, X_2, \ldots$ in two populations which are distinguished by the value of Y, as in **discriminant analysis**. If the distributions of X in each population are multivariate Normal, this analysis leads to relations that are formally equivalent to the logistic model, but the underlying view of the phenomena under review is quite different. We refer to Amemiya (1981) for details.

All the behavioural models reviewed above end up by giving $P(X)$ as the distribution function of a random disturbance term, which may or may not itself be defined as the difference of two other disturbances—see (28) or (33). Whether this yields the logistic or some other function depends on the probability distribution of these disturbances. We consider two common specifications in the next section.

2.3 Two common densities

Upon the introduction of the logistic function in Section 2.1 we have argued that, in addition to its analytical convenience, it has the right properties for a probability function: it increases monotonically from 0 to 1 as X ranges over the X-axis from one end to another, and the symmetry of (9) places the alternatives $Y = 1$ and $Y = 0$ on the same footing. These properties are however shared by the cumulative distribution function $F(.)$ of *any* random variable with a symmetric density function that allows for a linear transformation of its argument. We may therefore specify any such density for the random variable of the behavioural models of Section 2.2, and we shall always obtain a proper probability function $P(X)$ from its distribution function.

In practice only two densities are used in this manner. The first is the **logistic** density, which yields the logit model, and the second is the **Normal**, which leads to the **probit** model.

The major merit of the logistic density is that it leads to the logit model; we may as well derive it from this distribution function. If we consider the simplest form (7)

$$F(Z) = Pl(Z) = \exp Z/(1 + \exp Z) \tag{34}$$

we obtain

$$f(Z) = \exp Z/(1 + \exp Z)^2 \tag{35}$$

This is known as the logistic density, the sech^2 or the Fisk density.* I know of no

* For more details see Johnson and Kotz (1970), vol. 2, Ch. 20.

experiment or model which engenders this distribution naturally. The density (35) has mean zero and variance $\pi^2/3$, so that the **standardised** logistic distribution with zero mean and unit variance has the distribution function

$$F_1(X) = \exp \lambda X/(1 + \exp \lambda X)$$
$$\lambda = \pi/\sqrt{3} \approx 1.814 \tag{36}$$

Its density is

$$f_1(x) = \lambda \exp \lambda X/(1 + \exp \lambda X)^2 \tag{37}$$

The second preferred specification is a **Normal** distribution of ε, or equivalently of ε_1 and ε_2 of (24) and (25) (note that these need not be independent to lead to Normal ε). The Normal density in its **standardised** form with zero mean and unit variance is

$$Z(X) = \frac{1}{\sqrt{(2\pi)}} \exp -\tfrac{1}{2}X^2 \tag{38}$$

We denote the corresponding distribution function as

$$\Phi(X) = \frac{1}{\sqrt{(2\pi)}} \int_{-\infty}^{X} \exp(-\tfrac{1}{2}t^2)\,dt \tag{39}$$

The Normal density is of course a quite common specification for any residual or otherwise unknown random variable, and it has a direct intuitive appeal, if only because of its familiarity. If we assume Normal disturbances in any of the models of the last section, $P(X)$ is a Normal distribution function; by analogy to the notation $Pl(.)$ for the logistic function we denote it as $Pn(.)$. The model is then

$$P(X) = Pn(\alpha + \beta X) \tag{40}$$

with

$$Pn(Z) = \Phi(Z) \tag{41}$$

This is known as the **probit** model; historically, it precedes the logit model, as we recount in Section 2.8.

While the probit specification (40) is analytically less tractable than the logistic function (5), the two functions are quite similar in shape, as was first pointed out by Winsor (1932). This can be demonstrated in various ways; we use two.

First we consider the densities of the underlying random disturbances in standardised form with zero mean and unit variance, that is the logit and Normal densities (37) and (39). Figure 2.4 shows that both densities are symmetrical. The logit density has a higher peak in the middle than the Normal; at first it declines faster than the Normal, and then it slows down to the thicker tails that are often mentioned. But these begin to count only beyond two and a half standard deviations from the mean, where both densities already have quite small values.

Since we use both distributions as vehicles for probability models, we should,

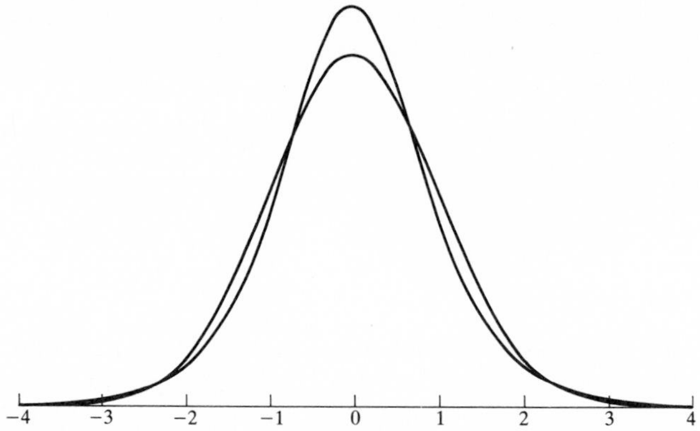

Fig. 2.4 Logistic and Normal density functions with zero mean and unit variance.

for considerations of fit, compare distribution functions rather than densities. The logistic has already been shown in Fig. 2.2, and one might contrast it with a Normal distribution function drawn to the corresponding scale in the same diagram; but it would then be virtually impossible to distinguish the two curves over most of the range. A numerical comparison is therefore in order.

We must first settle what adjustment of the coefficients of the transformations

$$Z = \alpha + \beta X$$

will render the two functions comparable, bearing in mind that in empirical work we very seldom consider probabilities outside the range from 0.1 to 0.9. Obviously, we should wish that the two functions Pl and Pn are both equal to 0.5 at the same value of X, which is equivalent to equating the means of the densities. The respective parameters α_l, β_l and α_n, β_n of the linear transformation of X must then satisfy

$$\alpha_l + \beta_l X^\circ = 0 \tag{42a}$$

$$\alpha_n + \beta_n X^\circ = 0 \tag{42b}$$

for the same value X°, or

$$\alpha_l/\beta_l = \alpha_n/\beta_n = X^\circ \tag{43}$$

In the present case, we complete the correspondence between the two functions by requiring the logistic distribution of

$$\alpha_l + \beta_l X$$

and the Normal distribution of

$$\alpha_n + \beta_n X$$

to have the same unit variance, as in Fig. 2.4. By (36) and (39) this leads to

$$\beta_l = \lambda \beta_n, \tag{44}$$

and hence, by (43),

$$\alpha_l = \lambda\alpha_n. \tag{45}$$

with λ equal to 1.814.

The result is shown in the first part of Table 2.1, where we have tabulated the two standardised distribution functions. Over the relevant range of the probabilities, the logit function is systematically somewhat steeper than the Normal. The second part of Table 2.1, which gives a tabulation of the inverse function, shows that with the present parameter ratio of 1.814 the argument of the logit is a little too small in absolute value. Over the range from 0.2 to 0.8 this amounts to just over 10%, and we should therefore use a ratio of very nearly 2 to bring about a closer correspondence over this middle region.

Table 2.1 Comparison of logit and probit probabilities.

A				B			
X	$F_l(X)$	$\Phi(X)$	Δ	P	Logit P	Probit P	Ratio
0	0.500	0.500	—	0.50	0	0	—
0.1	0.545	0.540	0.005	0.51	0.022	0.025	1.136
0.2	0.590	0.579	0.011	0.52	0.044	0.050	1.138
0.3	0.633	0.618	0.015	0.53	0.066	0.075	1.138
0.4	0.674	0.655	0.019	0.54	0.088	0.100	1.136
0.5	0.712	0.692	0.020	0.55	0.111	0.126	1.136
0.75	0.796	0.773	0.023	0.60	0.224	0.253	1.133
1.00	0.860	0.841	0.019	0.65	0.341	0.385	1.129
1.25	0.906	0.894	0.012	0.70	0.467	0.524	1.123
1.50	0.938	0.933	0.005	0.75	0.606	0.675	1.114
1.75	0.960	0.960	—	0.80	0.764	0.842	1.101
2.00	0.974	0.977	−0.003	0.85	0.956	1.036	1.084
2.25	0.983	0.988	−0.005	0.90	1.211	1.282	1.058
2.50	0.989	0.994	−0.005	0.95	1.623	1.645	1.013

Part A: for negative X take complements.
Part B: for complements of P, reverse signs.
Normal values from Fisher and Yates (1975).

This example shows that by judicious adjustment of the linear transformations of the argument X, the logit and probit probability functions can be made to coincide over a fairly wide range. Logit and probit functions which have been fitted to the same data are therefore virtually indistinguishable, and it is impossible to choose between the two on empirical grounds.* As for theoretical arguments, they have most force for multinomial models with more than two states; we postpone their discussion to Chapter 3.

* Finney (1971, p. 98) quotes an example. The ratio of logit coefficients to probit coefficients estimated by the primitive method of equations (69) and (72) below turns out to be 2.06, provided we change to natural logarithms and deduct the conventional 5 from the probits. This is close enough to the value of 2 given above.

2.4 Estimation from individual data: maximum likelihood

Probability models are as a rule estimated from survey data, which provide large samples of independent observations with a wide range of variation of the regressor variables. The preferred method of estimation is maximum likelihood. This permits the estimation of the parameters of almost any analytical specification of the probability function, and it yields estimates that are consistent and asymptotically efficient, together with ready estimates of their asymptotic covariance matrix. In the present context we can not go into the theory of this method, but we can show how it works.*

We first consider the general case of any probability model. The data from a sample survey consist of $i = 1, 2, \ldots, n$ observations on (a) the occurrence of a certain event or state, denoted by the (0,1) variable Y_i, and (b) a number of regressor variables $X_i, Z_i, \ldots$, which are arranged in the corresponding vector $\mathbf{x}_i$. The probability that observation i has $Y_i = 1$ is

$$P_i = P(\mathbf{x}_i, \boldsymbol{\theta}) \tag{46}$$

with any given specification of the function $P(.)$. Since successive observations are independent, the probability density of any given ordering of observed outcomes, say

$$1, 0, 1, 1, \ldots$$

is the product

$$P_1 . Q_2 . P_3 . P_4 \ldots$$

The sample density of a vector $\mathbf{y}$ of zeros and ones is therefore, written in full,

$$f(\mathbf{y}, \mathbf{X}, \boldsymbol{\theta}) = P(\mathbf{x}_1, \boldsymbol{\theta}) . Q(\mathbf{x}_2, \boldsymbol{\theta}) . P(\mathbf{x}_3, \boldsymbol{\theta}) . P(x_4, \boldsymbol{\theta}) . \cdots \tag{47}$$

where $\mathbf{X}$ denotes some convenient arrangement in a matrix of the n regressor vectors $\mathbf{x}_i$ and $Q_i(.)$ is the complement of $P_i(.)$. In this density, the sequence of outcomes $\mathbf{y}$ is the argument, $\boldsymbol{\theta}$ is a vector of unknown fixed parameters, and $\mathbf{X}$ (or the set of $\mathbf{x}_i$) consists of known constants. The **likelihood function** L of the sample has exactly the same form, but now the sequence of noughts and ones is fixed, as given by the sample observations, and $\boldsymbol{\theta}$ is the argument. The character of $\mathbf{X}$ does not change.

As L is a product, the **loglikelihood function** $\log L$ is a sum, and we may write it in several ways. One notation is

$$\log L(\boldsymbol{\theta}) = \sum_{i \varepsilon A_1} \log P(\mathbf{x}_i, \boldsymbol{\theta}) + \sum_{i \varepsilon A_0} \log Q(\mathbf{x}_i, \boldsymbol{\theta}) \tag{48}$$

where we have introduced the sets A_1 and A_0 for observations with Y equal to 1

* For the easiest introduction to the subject I could think of see Cramer (1986a).

and 0 respectively. Another way of writing $\log L$ is

$$\log L(\boldsymbol{\theta}) = \sum_i \{ Y_i \log P(\mathbf{x}_i, \boldsymbol{\theta}) + (1 - Y_i) \log Q(\mathbf{x}_i, \boldsymbol{\theta})\} \tag{49}$$

Note that the actual ordering of the observations is immaterial in either expression; since the observations are independent, the way they are ordered is arbitrary, and it does not affect their density nor the (log)likelihood.* The two expressions are of course identical; the first suggests an appealing layout of the calculations (but they are never performed by hand), while the second is more convenient in the derivations which follow below.

The maximum likelihood estimate or MLE of $\boldsymbol{\theta}$ is $\hat{\boldsymbol{\theta}}$, which maximises the likelihood or its logarithm; we find these values by equating the derivatives of $\log L$ to zero. By convention these derivatives form a row vector; transposition yields the **score vector q**, as in

$$(\partial \log L/\partial \boldsymbol{\theta})^{\mathrm{T}} = \mathbf{q} \tag{50}$$

with typical element

$$q_j = \partial \log L(\boldsymbol{\theta})/\partial \theta_j \tag{51}$$

The estimates $\hat{\boldsymbol{\theta}}$ are obtained by solving the system of equations

$$\mathbf{q}(\hat{\boldsymbol{\theta}}) = \mathbf{0} \tag{52}$$

As a rule these equations however have no analytical solution, and $\hat{\boldsymbol{\theta}}$ must be found by successive approximation. One way to do this is to expand $\mathbf{q}(\boldsymbol{\theta})$ around some given $\boldsymbol{\theta}^\circ$ in the neighbourhood of $\hat{\boldsymbol{\theta}}$ in a Taylor series. This yields

$$\mathbf{q}(\hat{\boldsymbol{\theta}}) \approx \mathbf{q}(\boldsymbol{\theta}^\circ) + \mathbf{Q}(\boldsymbol{\theta}^\circ)(\hat{\boldsymbol{\theta}} - \boldsymbol{\theta}^\circ) \tag{53}$$

where **Q** denotes the **Hessian** matrix of $\log L$, that is, the matrix of its second derivatives. Upon making use of (52) we find

$$\hat{\boldsymbol{\theta}} \approx \boldsymbol{\theta}^\circ - \mathbf{Q}(\boldsymbol{\theta}^\circ)^{-1}\mathbf{q}(\boldsymbol{\theta}^\circ) \tag{54}$$

Since this holds only approximately, it can not be used to determine $\hat{\boldsymbol{\theta}}$ from $\boldsymbol{\theta}^\circ$, but it does serve to obtain a closer approximation than $\boldsymbol{\theta}^\circ$. We thus use (54) as an iterative scheme, calculating the next approximation $\boldsymbol{\theta}_{t+1}$ from $\boldsymbol{\theta}_t$ by

$$\boldsymbol{\theta}_{t+1} = \boldsymbol{\theta}_t - \mathbf{Q}(\boldsymbol{\theta}_t)^{-1}\mathbf{q}(\boldsymbol{\theta}_t) \tag{55}$$

This is known as **Newton's method**, or the **Newton–Raphson method**, or as **quadratic hill-climbing**. The iterative scheme must of course still be completed by a **starting value**, say $\boldsymbol{\theta}_0$, and by a **convergence criterion** to determine when to stop; we discuss these presently.

* Purists may wish to add a combinatorial term to the density, and hence to the likelihood, to allow for the number of permutations of the ordered observations. This term, however, does not contain $\boldsymbol{\theta}$, so that it merely adds a constant to $\log L$; it is of no consequence for the maximisation of that function, and it can be safely ignored in the estimation of $\boldsymbol{\theta}$.

The Hessian **Q** has other uses as well. Its expected value with reverse sign is the Fisher **information matrix H**,

$$\mathbf{H} = -E\mathbf{Q} \tag{56}$$

where E is the expectation operator which takes the mathematical expectation of each element of **Q**. The inverse of **H** is the asymptotic covariance matrix of the MLE $\hat{\boldsymbol{\theta}}$

$$\mathbf{V}\hat{\boldsymbol{\theta}} = \mathbf{H}^{-1} \tag{57}$$

The elements of **Q**, **H** and **V** are in general functions of $\boldsymbol{\theta}$. We estimate them by substituting $\hat{\boldsymbol{\theta}}$; the estimated covariance matrix is thus

$$\hat{\mathbf{V}} = \mathbf{H}(\hat{\boldsymbol{\theta}})^{-1} \tag{58}$$

Recall that **H** is constructed according to (56). (Asymptotic) standard errors of the parameter estimates follow immediately by taking square roots of the diagonal elements. We can moreover obtain the variance (and hence the standard error) of any transformation of the estimated coefficients like the derivative (13) or the quasi-elasticity (15). For any reasonably well-behaved function $\phi(\hat{\boldsymbol{\theta}})$ of the estimates with covariance matrix $\mathbf{V}\hat{\boldsymbol{\theta}}$ we have

$$\operatorname{var}\phi = \boldsymbol{\phi}' V \boldsymbol{\phi}'^{\mathrm{T}} \tag{59}$$

where $\boldsymbol{\phi}'$ denotes the row vector of derivatives of ϕ in respect of $\boldsymbol{\theta}$. The estimated variance is of course obtained by evaluating the derivatives at $\hat{\boldsymbol{\theta}}$ and inserting $\hat{\mathbf{V}}$ for **V**.

Since we need **H** in the end, we may as well use it at an earlier stage, and substitute it into (55) which is after all only a means of generating successive approximations. This leads to the iterative scheme known as scoring, that is

$$\boldsymbol{\theta}_{t+1} = \boldsymbol{\theta}_t + \mathbf{H}(\boldsymbol{\theta}_t)^{-1}\mathbf{q}(\boldsymbol{\theta}_t) \tag{60}$$

The method has been attributed to Gauss and to Fisher.

In addition to (55) and (60), other iterative scheme can be devised to solve (52). In the case of the logit model, we prefer the scoring method of (60) because it leads to simple formulae. Even so, it should be appreciated that the elements of **Q**, **H** and **q** all consist of sums of n terms. As a rule these terms are functions of $\mathbf{x}_i$ and of $\boldsymbol{\theta}$. Since the $\mathbf{x}_i$ differ from one i to another, all n terms may have to be calculated anew at each round of the iterative process for the new set of working parameter values $\boldsymbol{\theta}_t$. The computations involved are therefore extensive, even if the formulae are simple.

All iterative schemes must be supplemented by **starting values** $\boldsymbol{\theta}_0$ for the parameter vector, and by a **convergence criterion** to stop the process. The judicious choice of starting values can contribute to speedy convergence of any iterative scheme, and the analyst will do well to use the occasion to think at some length about plausible values of the parameters. This exercise is of great help later when it comes to interpreting the final results. As for the **convergence**

criterion, the iterative process may be stopped (1) when $\log L$ ceases to increase perceptibily, (2) when the score vector comes quite close to zero, or (3) when successive parameter values are nearly equal. Most program packages employ default convergence criteria that are absurdly small in view of the precision of the data and of the statistical precision of the final point estimates. But this usually adds only a few more iterations at negligible computing cost.

From given starting values, the iterative scheme will run until convergence and then yield the following results:

- MLE $\hat{\boldsymbol{\theta}}$ of the parameter vector. Under quite general conditions these estimates are consistent, asymptotically efficient, and asymptotically Normal.
- Corresponding estimates of function of $\boldsymbol{\theta}$ like derivatives and quasi-elasticities, which are also MLE since a function of MLE is itself a MLE of the function.
- The (asymptotic) standard errors of the parameter estimates or of the estimated function values, derived from the estimate of their (asymptotic) covariance matrix (58), or from (59).
- The maximum value of the loglikelihood function, $\log L(\hat{\boldsymbol{\theta}})$.

The value of the loglikelihood function for particular sets of parameter estimates is useful when we wish to consider and test simplifying assumptions (like zero coefficients, or the absence of certain variables from the model), or more generally **restrictions** on the parameter vector $\boldsymbol{\theta}$. Provided the restricted model is **nested** as a special case within the general or **unrestricted** model, this can be tested by the **loglikelihood ratio** or **LR test**. The test statistic is

$$LR = 2(\log L(\hat{\boldsymbol{\theta}}_u) - \log L(\hat{\boldsymbol{\theta}}_r)) \qquad (61)$$

with u and r denoting unrestricted and restricted models respectively. Under the null hypothesis that the restriction holds, this statistic is asymptotically distributed as chi square with r degrees of freedom, equal to the number of (independent) restrictions on the parameter vector.*

So much for the general theory of maximum likelihood estimation. Before we implement it for probability models in general, and for the logit in particular, we must clear up the role of the regressor variables $\mathbf{x}_i$. These were last seen in the density (46) and in the loglikelihood functions (48) and (49), where they were described as 'known constants'. While they were dropped from the subsequent formulae, they are of course still present in the expressions for $\mathbf{q}$, $\mathbf{Q}$, and $\mathbf{H}$, and thus play an important role in the calculations.

The designation of the $\mathbf{x}_i$ as 'known constants' is ambiguous. In a laboratory experiment, the values of $\mathbf{x}_i$ are set by the analyst, in accordance with the rules of experimental design or otherwise, and they can validly be regarded as known nonrandom constants. In the case of a sample survey, however, this is not correct. Yet we can vindicate the use of the same formulae. We shall briefly sketch the argument, although the issue may seem of academic interest.

* This is the only test of a nested hypothesis we shall be using, but there are others. See Cramer (1986a), Ch. 3.

A proper description of a sample survey is to consider the sample observations as drawings from a joint distribution of $\mathbf{x}$ and Y, with a density $h(.)$ for a single observation. In this way we treat the sample regressor variables as random variables in their own right; they are sometimes called **covariates**. The joint density $h(.)$ can be rewritten as the product of the conditional density of Y and the marginal density of $\mathbf{x}$, or

$$h(Y, \mathbf{x}, \boldsymbol{\phi}) = f(Y, \mathbf{x}, \boldsymbol{\theta}) \,.\, g(\mathbf{x}, \zeta) \tag{62}$$

The extended parameter vector $\boldsymbol{\phi}$ comprises both $\boldsymbol{\theta}$ and ζ. Note that the conditional density $f(.)$ of Y corresponds to the probability (46). The marginal density of $\mathbf{x}$ reflects both the joint distribution of the variables concerned in the population and the operation of the sampling method. It is identical to the population density if the sampling is entirely random, but this is seldom the case. If there are strong suspicions that the sampling scheme distorts the population distribution because it is related to elements of $\mathbf{x}$—or even to the value of Y—we should spell out this explicitly, writing $h(.)$ itself as the product of the marginal distribution of characteristics in the population and of the conditional probability that an individual or household with certain characteristics is included in the sample.

If we now follow the same passage as before from the density of a single observation (62) to the density of the entire sample, from the density to the likelihood, and from the likelihood to the loglikelihood, the latter will be found to consist of the sum of two terms. The first represents $f(.)$ and is identical to the loglikelihood functions (48) and (49), and the second reflects $g(.)$. The total loglikelihood function for the sample $\log L^*$ is then

$$\log L^* = \log L(\boldsymbol{\theta}) + \sum_i \log g(\mathbf{x}_i, \zeta) \tag{63}$$

In the estimation of $\boldsymbol{\theta}$ by maximising this function in respect of $\boldsymbol{\theta}$ we may however omit the second term altogether. This brings us back to the same loglikelihood function that formed the basis of estimation before. That loglikelihood and the ensuing derivations therefore hold equally well for a survey as for experimental data, although for different reasons. The survey argument is generally known as 'conditioning on the covariates'.

Closer examination of (63) brings out two further observations. The first is that the same data we use for estimating the relationship between Y and $\mathbf{x}$ may also be informative about the distribution of $\mathbf{x}$ itself.* This should cause no surprise. If $\mathbf{x}$ is income, the same sample may be used to study the relation of car ownership to income as well as the income distribution. Most sample surveys are used for several analyses with different purposes.

The second point to note is that the argument for the use of the partial loglikelihood depends critically on the fact that the marginal distribution of $\mathbf{x}$

* In certain cases we may even go one step further and extract additional information about the distribution of $\mathbf{x}$ from the observed values of Y. See footnote on p. 28.

does not depend on $\boldsymbol{\theta}$, in other words that the sample values of $\mathbf{x}$ are independent of the values taken by Y. This important condition can easily be violated. If Y is car ownership and $\mathbf{X}$ is household income, we do not seriously envisage the possibility that income is affected by the presence or absence of a car. But the sampling scheme may be at fault if the probability that a household is included in the sample is affected by its car ownership status, which reflects its income level. This is known as **endogenous sample selection**, and it may for instance occur if the survey is inadvertently held among the customers of a supermarket which is so located that it is visited primarily by people with cars. Much more glaring instances of endogenous selection occur if a sample for the analysis of labour market histories is drawn from unemployment registers, or when medical records are obtained by sampling the patients of a hospital or clinic. At first sight, it would be advisable in the interest of a simple and straightforward statistical analysis to draw these samples before unemployment or illness occurs, for it is clear that the composition of the sample is distorted by the way it has been drawn; but this course is not always practicable. Endogenous selection may even be a matter of design, as when rare events or states are of particular interest. Even huge random samples would provide only a few relevant observations, and the analyst may well wish to base his conclusions on a sizeable group. The particular cases of interest are therefore over-represented, by drawing (additional) observations from suitable records, or by other selection mechanisms. A simple example is a two-stage sample design, where the first stage is a large random sample which merely serves to identify interesting individuals of a rare type, and the second is a proper survey which includes all these together with a sprinkling from the rest.

Whether endogenous sample selection is deliberate or not, it does distort the observed sample incidence of the alternatives under consideration. But distortion here means that the actual process whereby the observations have arisen is not properly represented by the density function underlying the likelihood function. The proper remedy is therefore to model the sampling process explicitly, and to allow for this in the density (62) and hence in the full loglikelihood function of the type of (63). It may be found that the distribution of $\mathbf{x}$ does depend on Y, and hence on $\boldsymbol{\theta}$, and this is then taken into account in deriving the MLE by maximising the likelihood function. We do not here pursue the subject further, but refer the reader to the work of Manski and Cosslett, who have treated the problem of estimation from deliberately choice-based samples in depth; see Manski and Lerman (1977), Manski and McFadden (1977b), Cosslett (1977, 1981) and Amemiya and Vuong (1987).

2.5 Estimation from individual data: implementation

We shall now apply the general method of maximum likelihood estimation to probability models in general, and to the logit model in particular.

First we take the loglikelihood function (49) of a probability model and derive expressions for $\mathbf{q}$, $\mathbf{Q}$ and $\mathbf{H}$, all in terms of the probabilities P_i and Q_i which are in turn functions of the parameters $\boldsymbol{\theta}$ (and of the known $\mathbf{x}_i$), though we omit these arguments. To begin with we find from (49), for the jth element of the score vector $\mathbf{q}$,

$$q_j = \partial \log L/\partial\theta_j = \sum_i \left\{\frac{Y_i}{P_i} - \frac{(1-Y_i)}{Q_i}\right\} \partial P_i/\partial\theta_j \tag{64}$$

For a typical element of $\mathbf{Q}$ we need the second derivative,

$$\begin{aligned} Q_{jk} &= \partial^2 \log L/\partial\theta_j\partial\theta_k \\ &= \sum_i \left\{\frac{Y_i}{P_i} - \frac{(1-Y_i)}{Q_i}\right\} \partial^2 P_i/\partial\theta_j\partial\theta_k - \sum_i \left\{\frac{Y_i}{P_i^2} + \frac{(1-Y_i)}{Q_i^2}\right\} \frac{\partial P_i}{\partial\theta_j}\cdot\frac{\partial P_i}{\partial\theta_k} \end{aligned} \tag{65}$$

For $\mathbf{H}$ we must reverse the sign and take the expected value of this expression, which leads to a considerable simplification. The only random variable is Y_i, and upon substituting $EY_i = P_i$ the first term of (65) vanishes altogether and the second is much simplified. We end up with

$$H_{jk} = \sum_i \frac{1}{P_i Q_i}\cdot\frac{\partial P_i}{\partial\theta_j}\cdot\frac{\partial P_i}{\partial\theta_k} \tag{66}$$

At this stage we introduce the logistic specification of the probability function, or, in the general form of (18),

$$\begin{aligned} P_i &= Pl(Z) = \exp X/(1 + \exp Z) \\ &= Pl(\mathbf{x}_i^{\mathrm{T}}\beta) = \exp \mathbf{x}_i^{\mathrm{T}}\beta/(1 + \exp \mathbf{x}_i^{\mathrm{T}}\beta) \end{aligned} \tag{67}$$

We have, by (13),

$$\mathrm{d}Pl_i/\mathrm{d}Z_i = Pl_i Ql_i \tag{68}$$

and

$$(\partial Z_i/\partial\beta)^{\mathrm{T}} = \mathbf{x}_i \tag{69}$$

As before, the transposition is in order since the derivatives of a scalar in respect of a vector are conventionally arranged in a row vector. When we substitute these expressions by the chain rule into (64) we obtain the score vector

$$\begin{aligned} \mathbf{q} &= \sum_i \left\{\frac{Y_i}{P_i} - \frac{(1-Y_i)}{Q_i}\right\} Pl_i Ql_i \mathbf{x}_i \\ &= \sum_i (Y_i Ql_i - (1-Y_i)Pl_i)\mathbf{x}_i \\ &= \sum_i (Y_i - Pl_i)\mathbf{x}_i \end{aligned} \tag{70}$$

Upon substitution of (68) and (69) into (65), we obtain an almost equally simple expression for the information matrix, namely

$$\mathbf{H} = \sum_i Pl_i Ql_i \mathbf{x}_i \mathbf{x}_i^{\mathrm{T}} \tag{71}$$

We recall that Pl_i and Ql_i are functions of the values assigned to the parameter vector $\boldsymbol{\theta}$ (as well as of the $\mathbf{x}_i$). Upon restoring these arguments in (70) and (71), and substituting the result in (60), we obtain the iterative scoring scheme written in full as

$$\boldsymbol{\theta}_{t+1} = \boldsymbol{\theta}_t + (\sum_i Pl_i(\boldsymbol{\theta}_t) Ql_i(\boldsymbol{\theta}_t) \mathbf{x}_i \mathbf{x}_i^{\mathrm{T}})^{-1} \cdot \sum_i (Y_i - Pl_i(\boldsymbol{\theta}_t)) \mathbf{x}_i \tag{72}$$

This expression gives substance to the iterative scoring method, and we now know how to compute the MLE of the logit model parameters by successive approximation.

The second term of (72), which represents $\boldsymbol{\theta}_{t1} - \boldsymbol{\theta}_t$, bears a close resemblance to the **normal equations** of OLS regression. If the observed regressor vectors $\mathbf{x}_i$ are arranged as the rows of a matrix X, we have

$$\sum_i \mathbf{x}_i \mathbf{x}_i^{\mathrm{T}} = \mathbf{X}^{\mathrm{T}}\mathbf{X} \tag{73}$$

The information matrix $\mathbf{H}$ of (71) therefore differs only by the weights $P_l Q_l$ from the matrix $\mathbf{X}^{\mathrm{T}}\mathbf{X}$, the sample moment matrix of the regressor variables in linear regression analysis, and many considerations from that model carry over.* To begin with, $\mathbf{X}$ must have full column rank, and strong but imperfect collinearity of the regressors will lead to a near-singular information matrix which implies large elements of the covariance matrix (57). In the present case, we have an additional interest in a well-conditioned matrix $\mathbf{H}$, since any numerical difficulties that may arise in its inversion will affect the speed and efficiency of the iterative process. Apart from not being near-singular, $\mathbf{X}^{\mathrm{T}}\mathbf{X}$ should preferably be well balanced in the sense that its elements do not vary too much in absolute size. This can be ensured by judicious scaling of the regressors.

Another point of similarity with linear regression is the role of the intercept. Once we have obtained the MLE $\hat{\boldsymbol{\theta}}$, we may predict the sample probabilities as

$$\hat{P}l_i = Pl(\mathbf{x}_i, \hat{\boldsymbol{\theta}}) \tag{74}$$

At the MLE $\hat{\boldsymbol{\theta}}$, the score vector must satisfy (52), so that by (70)

$$\sum_i (Y_i - \hat{P}l_i) \mathbf{x}_i = \mathbf{0} \tag{75}$$

If $\boldsymbol{\beta}$ contains an intercept, the $\mathbf{x}_i$ contain a unit element, and we therefore have

$$\sum_i (Y_i - \hat{P}l_i) = 0, \qquad \sum_i Y_i = \sum_i \hat{P}l_i \tag{76}$$

The predicted sample frequency is therefore equal to the actual sample

* Note that the solution of (72) can not be represented as a weighted linear regression problem, since the weights $Pl_i(\boldsymbol{\theta}) Ql_i(\boldsymbol{\theta})$ depend on the parameter values, and must be adjusted in every round of the iterative process.

frequency, just as the predicted mean of a regression equation equals the observed mean.

This last result will also hold for a logit model with an intercept only, that is the **base line model** that we use as a benchmark in an LR test of the significance of a set of regressors. In this model, the argument $x_i^T\beta$ of (18) and (67) consists of a constant α° only, and the same probabilities

$$Pl^\circ = \exp\alpha^\circ/(1 + \exp\alpha^\circ) \tag{77a}$$

$$Ql^\circ = 1 - Pl^\circ = 1/(1 + \exp\alpha^\circ) \tag{77b}$$

apply to all observations. By (76), maximum likelihood estimation of α° will yield

$$\hat{P}l^\circ = \sum_i Y_i/n = m/n = f \tag{78}$$

with m the number of sample observations with the attribute under review, and f its relative frequency in the sample. It follows that

$$\begin{aligned}\hat{\alpha}^\circ &= R(\hat{P}l^\circ) = \log \hat{P}l^\circ/\hat{Q}l^\circ = \log(f/(1-f)) \\ &= \log m - \log(n - \mathrm{m})\end{aligned} \tag{79}$$

By (48), the corresponding **base line loglikelihood** is

$$\begin{aligned}\log L^\circ &= m\log f + (n-m)\log(1-f) \\ &= m\log m + (n-m)\log(n-m) - n\log n\end{aligned} \tag{80}$$

This can be regarded as a restricted version of any argument $\mathbf{x}_i^T\boldsymbol{\beta}$, with all regression coefficients except the intercept constrained to equal zero. The corresponding LR test statistic (61) is

$$\mathrm{LR}^\circ = 2(\log L(\hat{\beta}) - \log L^\circ) \tag{81}$$

and under the null hypothesis that the regressor variables have no effect this has a chi square distribution with $(k - 1)$ degrees of freedom.

In the practice of estimation, the reader will probably make no use of the above algebra, and prefer the logit option of some standard estimation program package. But there is no harm in understanding what is going on, and the above formulae moreover show that it does not require superhuman efforts to write a computer program of one's own. A specific program is usually more efficient than the logit option of a more general package.

The iterative scheme (72) must still be supplemented by **starting values** $\boldsymbol{\theta}_0$ of the parameters, and by a **convergence criterion** to stop the process. The general remarks about these matters at the end of Section 2.4 apply, but we can be a little more specific about starting values. It will be shown that for the logit model the scoring algorithm will always converge to a single maximum in the end, so that any starting value will do: its choice is important only for the speed of convergence.* Setting all parameters equal to zero implies that the probabilities

* See Section 3.5, equ. (3.57), for the convergence property.

in the first round are all equal to 0.5, which is not a bad start. An alternative, used by most program packages, is to put all coefficients at zero save the intercept, which is then estimated in the first round by (79).

Other starting values of the β_j can be obtained by setting a reasonable value for the quasi-elasticity η of (15) at the sample mean $\bar{X}_j$, and again substituting f for the probability; β_{jo} is then obtained by solving

$$\eta(\bar{X}) \approx f(1-f)\beta_{jo}\bar{X}_j \qquad (82)$$

for the assumed value of $\eta(\bar{X})$.

With reasonable data and a reasonable computer program convergence should be achieved in something like five or, at the outside, ten iterations. If the number is much larger, something is wrong. First, the data may be ill conditioned, with an almost singular regressor matrix; with regressors of widely different order of magnitude; or with a sample frequency of the attribute under consideration very close to 0 or 1, and a consequent lack of variation in the value of Y_i. If there is collinearity of the regressors, one or two can be omitted; if the regressors show too little variation, others may be sought and found; and if the regressor matrix is simply unbalanced we may scale the variables. But if the incidence of the attribute varies too little, nothing can be done. Secondly, but very unlikely, extremely awkward starting values may have been chosen; this is easily remedied. The convergence criterion is seldom at fault, for even if it is much too strict by any reasonable standard this will seldom cause a large number of unnecessary iterations. But the matter is easily put right. The criterion built into a program package can usually be circumvented by making the program print out the value of $\log L$ and of the parameters at each iteration, and stopping the process by hand intervention when these statistics cease to vary in successive iterations.

2.6 Estimation from grouped data

Survey data often contain variables that are restricted to a limited number of values set by convention. This applies to genuine (0,1) variables like gender or nationality, but also to 'level of education' or 'degree of urbanisation'. Like some dependent variables, many regressor variables that are quite capable of continuous variation may be limited to a few broad classes by the choice of the analyst or by the method of measurement and recording. For items like urbanisation and education it makes sense to adopt the standard classification, and sensitive items like income are sometimes discreetly determined by showing the respondents a printed card with a number of broad income classes, and asking them to indicate their positions. If **all** regressor variables of relevance are of this **categorical type**, we may set up a complete cross tabulation of the sample with a limited number of cells. The total sample information is then summarised by the number of observations with and without the dependent attribute for each cell. As we shall see, such **grouped observations** permit a greater choice of methods of estimation.

We denote by $j = 1, 2, \ldots, J$ the cells defined by the cross-classification of the sample by categorical regressors. The number of observations in each cell is n_j, the number with the dependent attribute under review m_j, and the number without l_j; clearly

$$n_j = m_j + l_j \qquad \text{for all } j \tag{83}$$

The **relative frequency** of the attribute in cell j is

$$f_j = m_j/n_j \tag{84}$$

The regressor variables take a single value for each cell; these values may be (0,1) dummies, or mid-class values of income classes, as the case may be. For each cell there is a single set of regressor values which forms the vector $\mathbf{x}_j$, and the within-cell variation (if any) of the regressors or covariates is ignored.*

A straightforward method of estimation is to regard the grouped observations simply as **repeated individual observations**, and to apply the maximum likelihood method of the preceding section. This is merely a matter of adjusting the notation. From (70) we find for the score vector

$$\begin{aligned} \mathbf{q} &= \sum_j (m_j - n_j Pl_j(\boldsymbol{\theta}))\mathbf{x}_j \\ &= \sum_j n_j(f_j - Pl_j(\boldsymbol{\theta}))\mathbf{x}_j \end{aligned} \tag{85}$$

The equivalent of the maximum condition (52) is therefore

$$\sum_j n_j(f_j - \hat{P}l_j)\mathbf{x}_j = \mathbf{0} \tag{86a}$$

with

$$\hat{P}l_j = Pl(\mathbf{x}_j, \hat{\boldsymbol{\theta}}) \tag{86b}$$

Note that each discrepancy $(f_j - \hat{P}l_j)$ will tend to zero as all n_j increase along with the sample size: it is basic sampling theory that f_j converges to Pl_j, and $\hat{P}l_j$ converges to Pl_j since $\hat{\boldsymbol{\theta}}$ is a consistent estimate of $\boldsymbol{\theta}$, and therefore $\hat{P}l_j$ is a consistent estimate of Pl_j. For $\mathbf{H}$ of (71) we find

$$\mathbf{H} = \sum_j n_j Pl_j Ql_j \mathbf{x}_j \mathbf{x}_j^{\mathrm{T}} \tag{87}$$

Together, (85) and (87) provide the necessary expressions for implementing the

* For grouped continuous variables like income, the class values are usually identified by mid-class values, with some *ad hoc* adjustment for the open-ended classes at either end. For the wider issue of whether we should allow for the within-class income variation (and make use of the information about this contained in the observed Y) see Cramer (1986b). It turns out that this can indeed be safely neglected.

scoring algorithm (60), viz.

$$\boldsymbol{\theta}_{t+1} = \boldsymbol{\theta}_t + \mathbf{H}(\boldsymbol{\theta}_t)^{-1}\mathbf{q}(\boldsymbol{\theta}_t)$$

A different approach is to consider the standard chi square statistic for testing whether an observed frequency distribution agrees with a given probability distribution. The general formula of this classical Pearson goodness of fit test is

$$\text{chi}^2 = \sum_k \frac{(s_k - \hat{s}_k)^2}{\hat{s}_k} \tag{88}$$

where s_k and $\hat{s}_k$ denote the observed and the predicted frequencies in class or interval k. This nonnegative quantity has a chi square distribution with (K − l) degrees of freedom, with K the number of cells and l the number of adjusted parameters that enter into the predicted numbers. For large values we must reject the null hypothesis that the s_k are a sample from the given distribution. This test is treated in most standard textbooks of statistics; see, for example, Mood *et al.* (1974, p. 442–448).

In the present case the predicted frequencies are those given by a logit model with estimated or assumed parameter values. We first consider a single cell of the cross-classification of the grouped data. With two classes only (with and without the attribute), the test statistic for this single cell is

$$\text{chi}_j^2 = \frac{(m_j - \hat{m}_j)^2}{\hat{m}_j} - \frac{(l_j - \hat{l}_j)^2}{\hat{l}_j} \tag{89}$$

or, after some rearrangement

$$\text{chi}_j^2 = n_j \frac{(f_j - \hat{f}_j)^2}{\hat{f}_j(1 - \hat{f}_j)} \tag{90}$$

We may sum these independent statistics over all cells to

$$\text{chi}^2 = \sum_j n_j \frac{(f_j - \hat{f}_j)^2}{\hat{f}_j(1 - \hat{f}_j)} \tag{91}$$

For large values of this statistic we must reject the null hypothesis that the observed cell samples with and without the attribute have been drawn from the dichotomous distributions prescribed by the logit model; we shall use the test in this manner in Section 5.5. In reverse, we may take (91) as a criterion function that must be minimised, and obtain **minimum chi square estimates** of $\boldsymbol{\theta}$. This estimator is not identical to the maximum likelihood estimator, although the two share the same asymptotic properties; see Rao (1955). It has been advocated with some vehemence by Berkson (1980) who stresses its superior small-sample qualities.

Provided f_j does not attain its bounds of zero or one, we may apply the log odds ratio (11), originally defined as a transformation of a probability, to this relative frequency. This is the original **logit** transformation of relative frequencies, defined as

$$\text{logit}(f_j) = \log(f_j/(1 - f_j)) \tag{92}$$

Insofar as f_j is approximately equal to P_j, and P_j equal to the logistic function $Pl(\mathbf{x}_j'\beta)$, we have, as in (12)

$$\text{logit}(f_j) \approx \mathbf{x}_j^{\mathrm{T}}\beta \tag{93}$$

This immediately suggests a linear regression equation for the transformed frequencies,

$$\text{logit}(f_j) = \mathbf{x}_j^{\mathrm{T}}\boldsymbol{\beta} + \varepsilon_j \tag{94}$$

This permits the estimation of $\boldsymbol{\beta}$ by linear regression methods. With ordinary least squares, it provides a fair first approximation for $\boldsymbol{\beta}$, although it will be clear that the implied standard assumptions about the error term ε_j are at variance with the underlying model. This can to some extent be remedied by allowing for heteroscedasticity; but linear regression estimation will always remain imperfect, and improvements beyond OLS impair the simplicity of the method which is its major attraction.

The same approach can be used for estimating the probit model of (40) and (41). While there is no simple analytical expression for the inverse of the Normal probability function $\Phi(Z)$ of (39) we may of course find the argument Z that belongs to any given value of Φ by consulting the standard table of the Normal probability integral at the back of most textbooks of statistics. It is this inverse transformation which was called the **probit**, defined by

$$\text{probit}(\Phi(Z)) = Z \qquad \text{for } 0 < Z < 1 \tag{95}$$

Once we have a tabulation of this transformation, we may apply it to observed frequencies.* As above, the transformed values can then be entered into a regression to estimate the parameters of (40), viz.

$$\text{probit}(f_j) = \alpha + \beta X_j + \varepsilon_j \tag{96}$$

Before the advent of electronic computing, probit and logit parameters were often established in this manner. With a single regressor variable, logit (f_j) can be plotted against X_j, and a straight line fitted by eye, or a regression of logits on the $\mathbf{x}_j$ may be run on the basis of (94), with or without further embellishments, like a correction for heteroscedasticity. The same holds for the probit transformation; see, for example, the discussion by Aitchison and Brown (1957, p. 31–4). Here one could even use graph paper with a special grid to plot relative frequencies against the regressor values. By now these methods are obsolete, although they do permit a quick and easy screening of grouped data and sometimes provide

* See Fisher and Yates (1957), Table IX, for an example. In these standard tables, the probits were habitually increased by 5 to avoid negative values and thus to facilitate the calculations for the regression (96); at the time, these were usually carried out by hand.

excellent starting values for the more sophisticated iterative schemes. Graphical inspection should not be despised; it has substantial instructive value.

2.7 Private car ownership and household income

We illustrate the logit model by an application to the ownership of private cars in the household budget survey of 1980 of the Dutch Central Bureau of Statistics. This survey provides extensive and detailed information about income and expenditure of a sample of over 2800 households. We shall use only a small fraction of this rich material, namely the information about car ownership, household income, family size, urbanisation and age. There is a great deal of information about car ownership (or rather about the cars at the disposal of the household), giving the number of cars, their age, other characteristics, etc., but we here only use the major distinction between *business cars* and *private cars*. Business cars are primarily used for business or professional purposes, regardless of whether they are paid for wholly or in part by the employer, or tax-deductible; all other cars are denoted here as private cars. Throughout the various analyses that we use as illustrations we shall concentrate on the choice of the household in the matter of private car ownership, and use the presence of a business car at most as a determining variable, along with the income level, family size and so on. The underlying idea is that business cars are a necessity of life (although they are available for private purposes), and that they are not subject to the same choice process as private cars.

In the present section we consider a simple logit model for private car ownership as a function of household income as the single explanatory variable. The attribute **private car ownership** covers the ownership of any number of private cars, regardless of their age or condition, and also regardless of the simultaneous ownership (or non-ownership) of business cars. The regressor variable X is the **logarithm** of **household income per equivalent adult**, or log of income per head, with the number of heads calculated by a weighting scheme which attaches less weight to children than to adults. The idea is that this reflects the needs of the household better than its size measured by the number of persons. The reason why we use the logarithm of income, and not income itself, is that it yields substantially better results, as indicated by a much higher value of the loglikelihood at its maximum. Experience shows that in these analyses direct stimuli like income are usually best measured on a logarithmic scale.*

We thus estimate a simple model with Y private car ownership and X the log of household income per head. This is the model of equations (1), (4), (7) and (9), or, summarizing these equations,

$$Y_i = 1 \text{ if household } i \text{ owns private car} \tag{97a}$$

$$Y_i = 0 \text{ otherwise} \tag{97b}$$

* See the passage about the logarithmic transformation in Section 2.2.

$$P_i = Pr(Y_i = 1) \tag{98a}$$
$$Q_i = \Pr(Y_i = 0) = 1 - P_i \tag{98b}$$

$$P_i = P(X_i) = Pl(\alpha + \beta X_i) \tag{99}$$

After omitting a number of households with incomplete records of car ownership status or income, the 1980 Dutch budget survey yields 2820 households with proper observations. Estimation is by the scoring method of (60), as embodied in the computer program LOGITJD. Three iterations are sufficient to attain convergence and we illustrate their course in Table 2.2.

Table 2.2 Estimation of a simple logit model of private car ownership (Dutch Budget Survey of 1980, $n = 2820$).

Iteration	log L	α	β	$\lvert q_\alpha \rvert$	$\lvert q_\beta \rvert$
0	−1839.63	0.3834	0	$<10^{-11}$	48.25
1	−1831.29	−2.7420	0.3441	2.30	22.72
2	−1831.29	−2.7723	0.3476	0.0016	0.0166
3	−1831.29	−2.7723	0.3476	$<10^{-8}$	$<10^{-7}$
		(3.35)*	(4.03)*		

* Absolute value of asymptotic t-values in brackets.

The first line or iteration zero shows the starting values with α_0 given by the base line estimate α° of (79) and β_0 equal to zero. In a diagram like Fig. 2.2 this would correspond to a straight horizontal line at the level of the average sample frequency of 0.65. In the next iterations the loglikelihood increases, the coefficients are adjusted, and the elements of the scoring vector $\mathbf{q}$ converge toward zero. Convergence is reached in only three iterations, but then the loglikelihood at its maximum is not so very much larger than at the zero iteration. In the final line we have made use of the asymptotic standard errors, obtained from the asymptotic covariance matrix, to calculate t-values. These ratios of the

Table 2.3 Private car ownership by income classes.

Limits of Class j	x_j^*	n_j	m_j	f_j
<10	7	400	220	0.55
10–15	13	962	627	0.65
15–25	20	992	636	0.64
25–35	28	330	227	0.69
⩾35	40	136	100	0.74

* Income per equivalent adults × Fl. 1000 per annum, in all calculations: Fl. per annum. Assigned class means.

estimates to their standard errors are shown, in absolute value, in brackets below the estimates to which they refer.

We shall shortly comment on the statistical and economic features of the estimation results. First, however, we illustrate estimation from grouped data by the very same data. The households have now been grouped into five classes according to their income per equivalent adult, and the entire sample information thus condensed is contained in Table 2.3.* We have assigned mid-class values, with some adjustments, to the classes, and use their logarithms as the regressor. Maximum likelihood estimation according to Section 2.6, equations (85) and following, treating the group values as if they were repeated individual observations, yields the results of Table 2.4. We arrive at much the same estimates as from the individual observations, again in three iterations, and the maximum value attained by the loglikelihood function is also not very much different.

Table 2.4 Estimation of car ownership model from grouped data of Table 2.3.

Iteration	$\log L$	α	β	$\lvert q_\alpha \rvert$	$\lvert q_\beta \rvert$
0	−1839.63	0.5834	0	$<10^{-13}$	48.38
1	−1830.89	−2.9184	0.3617	2.4144	23.33
2	−1830.88	−2.9153	0.3618	0.0013	0.0124
3	−1830.88	−2.9154	0.3618	$<10^{-9}$	$<10^{-8}$
		(3.48)	(4.17)		

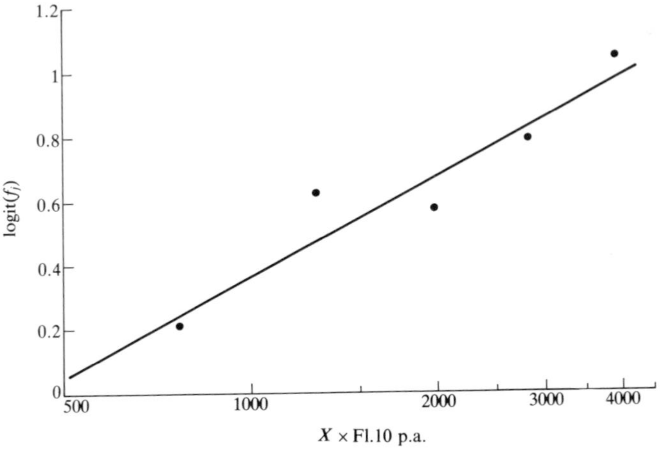

Fig. 2.5 Logit of car ownership frequency plotted against log of income per head, data of Table 2.3.

* The classification of households by classes of income per equivalent adult is highly unusual. We use it here since we want grouped data with the same regressor variable as the individual data.

Finally, the logit transformation (92) may be applied to the relative frequencies from the last column of Table 2.3. The resulting values are plotted against the logarithm of mid-class income in Fig. 2.5. Upon fitting a straight line by eye and reading off its slope and the abscissa of the intersection with the X-axis we find

$$\alpha = -3.60, \qquad \beta = 0.43$$

This not so close to the estimates of Table 2.2 as the grouped data estimates, but still within reasonable bounds. Note that this technique does not provide a standard error of the estimate. It only serves to inspect the data and to find starting values for an iterative algorithm.

So much for a comparison of the different techniques of estimation for the simple case of a single regressor variable. They yield virtually the same results, but these results in themselves are disappointing. We notice that the value of $\log L$ does not improve much beyond the zero iteration, which is the **base line** model of fitting a constant probability, with the estimate of (79) and the loglikelihood of (80). The small improvement of $\log L$ over this base line value $\log L^\circ$ suggests that income does little or perhaps nothing to explain private car ownership. We test the restrictive hypothesis of zero β by the LR test (81). Upon comparing the final loglikelihood of Table 2.2 to the base-line value, we find a test statistic of 16.68. With one degree of freedom, this is quite significant, for the 5% critical value of chi quare is 3.84. The absence of any income effect is thus rejected. As a matter of fact, the estimated income coefficient of Table 2.2 differs significantly from zero by its t-ratio of 4.05.

But this purely statistical reassurance does not remedy the fact that the influence of income alone on private car ownership as here defined is small. This is clearly demonstrated by the grouped data of Table 2.3, with car ownership incidence varying only within narrow bounds from one income class to another. The result is that we find very low income coefficients, with all that this implies.* The estimates from Table 2.2 imply that fifty per cent ownership is reached at a value of $2.77/0.35 = 7.98$ for logincome, or around Fl. 3000 per equivalent adult, which is an absurdly low value; but this is due to the combination of an average sample frequency of over 0.5 and a very small income coefficient. Since the income variable is in logarithms, the quasi-elasticity of private car ownership in respect of income is given by the derivative (13); at the sample mean ownership rate of 65%, this gives

$$0.35 \times 0.65 \times 0.35 = 0.08,$$

which is much lower than one would expect: a 12% rise in income is needed to increase the probability of car ownership by one percentage point. Insofar as the sample mean is merely used as a convenient point for evaluating statistics, its random character can be ignored; the transformation of β to a derivative (or a

* Another consequence of the limited variation of relative ownership frequencies between income classes, combined with an anomalous value in income class 3, is that the grouped data estimates are quite sensitive to the exact values of the 'mid-class' incomes assigned to each class.

quasi-elasticity, or an elasticity) then involves no other random variables, and the t-ratio of 4.05 of β applies to 0.08 as well.

We conclude that by purely statistical assessment the income effect is significantly different from zero, but that by economic considerations it is absurdly small. This conclusion was already apparent from Fig. 2.5; to demonstrate the fact once more, we reproduce the fitted curve of car ownership as a function of income per head in Fig. 2.6. Note that the use of the logarithmic transformation for income renders the shape of the sigmoid curve asymmetrical. In the present case, the major conclusion is that the slope of the curve is very weak.

There are two reasons for this low income effect; the first is a valid explanation of why it is lower than one would expect, the other points to a downward bias of the estimated coefficient that must be remedied. The first argument is that the income elasticity of ownership is so small because the ownership rate is so high. We saw in Table 2.3 that even among the lowest income class the ownership rate exceeds 50%; with an overall mean rate of 65%, the higher income groups rapidly approach the saturation owership level of 100%, and there is not much room for a further rise. In general, ownership rates are sooner affected by saturation than the volume of consumer demand, and this volume is sooner saturated than money expenditure. While household expenditure on motoring may well be a luxury with an income elasticity in excess of one, even after quite high levels have been attained, this will take the form of the purchase of more expensive cars, or of the ownership of more than one car, rather than in the ownership rate we consider here.

The second point, equally important, is that the coefficient β is severely biased by the omission of other relevant variables from the analysis. Unlike regression coefficients, logit model coefficients suffer from bias towards zero upon the neglect of additional explanatory variables, as we shall explain and illustrate in the next section.

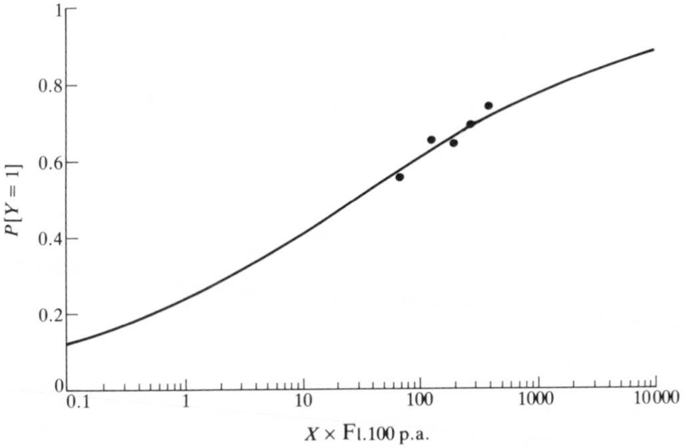

Fig. 2.6 Fitted probability of car ownership as a function of income per head.

2.8 Further analysis of private car ownership

We shall now add several other regressor variables to income, or rather to the log of income per equivalent adult (denoted at LINCEQ), namely

- LSIZE, the log of household size, measured by the number of equivalent adults;
- BUSCAR, a (0,1) dummy variable for the presence of a business car in the household;
- URBA, the degree of urbanisation, measured on a six-point scale from the countryside (1) to the city (6);
- HHAGE, the age of the head of household, measured by five-year classes, starting with the class 'below 20'.

For most of these variables, the definition has been dictated by the data set; we have some misgivings about measuring household size in equivalent adults, not in persons, but the latter variable was not available in the data to which we had access.

We shall show that the addition of significant regressor variables improves the fit, increases the precision of the estimates, and gradually corrects the **omitted variables bias** that occurs for all coefficients if relevant determinants are not included in the analysis.

This bias occurs in probability models and we shall demonstrate it for the logit model. It constitutes a major departure from the properties of the standard linear regression model. In that model, the neglect of omitted regressor variables does not affect the remaining coefficient estimates and merely shows up in an increased residual variance, provided the omitted regressors are uncorrelated with the retained regressors.* In the logit model, however, the exclusion of relevant variables from the argument biases the estimates of the remaining slope coefficients towards zero.

To see this, recall the justification of the probability model from the dispersion of some underlying threshold value among individuals. In that argument of Section 2.2, equations (29) and (30), the slope of the probability curve is inversely related to the dispersion of individual tolerance levels: the larger this dispersion, the smaller (in absolute value) is the slope of the distribution function. If we add another regressor variable, this is equivalent to controlling for an additional factor, reducing the dispersion, and increasing the slope. In the extreme case where all variability is accounted for by regressor variables, the probability function for a subgroup of truly homogeneous individuals with identical behaviour would no longer be sigmoid but a simple step function.

As an example we consider the case of two subsamples of large households and small households respectively, with distinct but parallel probability functions for private car ownership, as shown in Fig. 2.7. This might, for example, be a logit model with a constant, income, and a (0,1) dummy variable for household size as

* See e.g. Johnston (1984), p. 260–1.

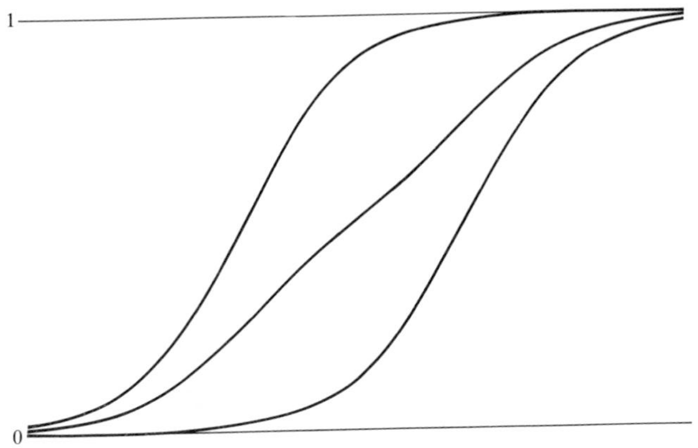

Fig. 2.7 Two parallel probability functions and average probability curve.

the regressor variables. If we now disregard household size, the average probability curve will be some sort of weighted average of the two separate curves, and it will inevitably have a weaker slope than its constituent parts. In probability models, omitted variables, residual variation or heterogeneity will thus always bias the estimated effects towards zero.

We may complete this intuitive argument by a more formal derivation. Let the true model that has generated the sample data be the logit function

$$P(Y_i = 1) = Pl(\alpha + \beta X_i + W_i) \tag{100}$$

where W_i describes the effect of one or more omitted variables. We shall treat this as if it were a random variable with zero mean and variance σ^2; any nonzero mean will be absorbed by α or its estimated value $\hat{\alpha}$. We now develop (100) into a Taylor series, retaining the second-order term, or

$$\begin{aligned} Pl(\alpha + \beta X_i + W_i) = Pl(\alpha + \beta X_i) + Pl'(\alpha + \beta X_i)W_i \\ + \tfrac{1}{2}Pl''(\alpha + \beta X_i)W_i^2 \end{aligned} \tag{101}$$

The probability of actually observing $Y_i = 1$ conditional upon X_i (but not on W_i!) is obtained by taking the expected value of this expression over W_i. In the interest of brevity we omit the familiar argument $\alpha + \beta X_i$ and write $Pl(*)$ for $Pl(\alpha + \beta X_i)$. The result is

$$\begin{aligned} P(Y_i = 1 | X_i) = Pl(*) \\ + \tfrac{1}{2}\sigma^2 Pl(*)(1 - Pl(*))(1 - 2Pl(*)) \end{aligned} \tag{102}$$

The last term indicates the bias of the observed Y_i, from which we shall estimate α and β when we fail to use W_i as a regressor. Its behaviour for $Pl(*)$ ranging from 0 to 1 is shown in Fig. 2.8. Clearly, its sign depends on the sign of $1 - 2Pl(*)$; if $Pl(*)$ is below 0.5, $P(Y_i = 1 | X_i)$ will be higher, and if $Pl(*)$ lies beyond 0.5 the probability of observing $Y_i = 1$ will be smaller. Over a fairly broad range from 0.1

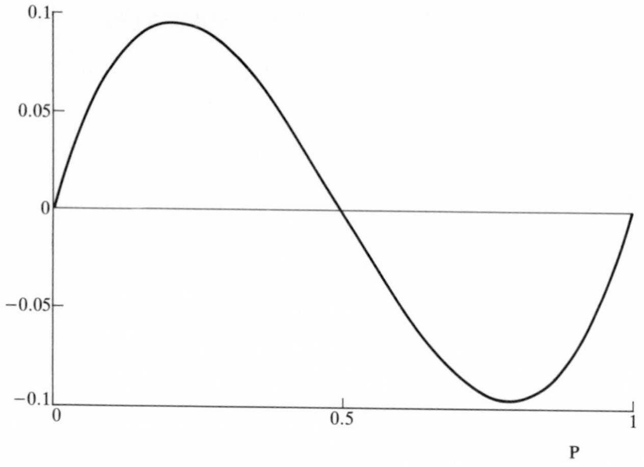

Fig. 2.8 Behaviour of $P(1-P)(1-2P)$.

to 0.4 the values of $Pl(*)$ are increased, and between 0.6 and 0.9 they are reduced; the size of these distortions depends on σ^2. On balance, the overall effect is to reduce the higher, and to increase the lower probabilities, so that the slope of expected probability as a function of X_i is reduced. As a result, the slope coefficient that is estimated from the observed values is biased towards zero. The argument can easily be extended to the case of several regressor variables: whenever relevant variables are omitted, all the estimated slope coefficients will be biased towards zero. We shall see in Section 3.6, however, that it does not hold for multinomial models with more than two states.

Table 2.5 Effect of adding regressor variables on loglikelihood of multinomial car ownership model.*

log *L*	LINC	LSIZE	BUSCAR	URBA	HHAGE
−1831.29	0.08				
	(4.0)				
−1614.92	0.41	0.51			
	(14.1)	(18.7)			
−1393.74	0.57	0.71	−0.68		
	(16.7)	(21.6)	(18.9)		
−1386.06	0.57	0.70	−0.69	−0.03	
	(16.7)	(21.1)	(19.0)	(3.9)	
−1351.39	0.55	0.63	−0.70	−0.03	−0.03
	(16.2)	(19.1)	(19.6)	(4.2)	(8.2)

* Derivatives, with asymptotic *t*-ratio, in absolute value, in brackets. Same data as Table 2.2

To show how this works in practice, we have successively added all the variables listed above to the simple analysis of income alone of the preceding section. Table 2.5 shows how the maximum loglikelihood increases upon the addition of each new variable, as is only natural. Whether these increases are *significant* can be tested by the likelihood ratio test of (61), for at each stage the simpler model is a restricted form of the extended model, with one coefficient equal to zero; since chi square with one degree of freedom is significant at the 5% level when it exceeds 3.84, the loglikelihoods should increase by at least half of this, or by 1.92. All additional variables pass this test, with URBA giving the weakest performance. It also stands to reason that the precision of the estimates, as reflected in their *t*-values, increases with each additional regressor.

Table 2.5 also shows the effect of introducing additional variables on the estimated slope coefficients, here represented by derivatives (equivalent to quasi-elasticities in the case of LINCEQ and LSIZE). We note an increase in their absolute level, away from zero, that is roughly in line with the increase in $\log L$; this is due to the reduction of the omitted variable bias. The effect of just adding a size variable on the quasi-elasticity of income is spectacular, for it leaps from 0.08 to 0.41, with a further advance to 0.57 when the presence of a business car is taken into account. From the third line on, the improvement of $\log L$ as well as the changes in the slope are less pronounced.

We end up with a quasi-elasticity of private car ownership in respect of income of 0.55, which is much more satisfactory than the earlier value of 0.08. The quasi-elasticity in respect of household size, as measured by the number of equivalent adults, is 0.63; note that this is a pure size effect, measured at a given income *per head*, and therefore considerably higher than the effect of an increase in family size at a given household income. The presence of a business car is the third important determinant: it reduces the probability of private car ownership by 70 percentage points. Given the overall level of the probability of private car ownership, a business car is to all intents a perfect substitute for a private car. The two remaining variables are less important determinants of car ownership, as their *t*-values indicate. Moving up one step in urbanisation, as measured on a six-class scale, reduces the probability of private car ownership by 3 percentage points, and so does a higher age of the head of household by five years.

2.9 The history of the logit model

The logit model as currently employed in econometric analysis stems from three distinct and separate sources: applied mathematics, experimental statistics, and economic theory. The **logistic function** was designed as early as 1845 as a **growth curve**; the bivariate **probability model**, initially identified exclusively with the Normal probit model, dates from biological statistics of the 1930s; and the theory of **discrete choice** or **random utility** arose as part of abstract economic theory around 1950. The full development of the generalised logit model dates from its use in traffic analysis in the early 1970s. We shall briefly review this curious history and sketch the largely fortuitous interaction between these three major strands.

Growth curves were originally designed to describe the development of a living population over time. Let $N(t)$ denote population size at time t, and $\dot{N}(t)$ its rate of absolute growth, or

$$\dot{N}(t) = \mathrm{d}N(t)/\mathrm{d}t \tag{103}$$

The simplest assumption to make is that $\dot{N}(t)$ is proportional to $N(t)$, or

$$\dot{N}(t) = \alpha N(t), \qquad \alpha = \dot{N}(t)/N(t) \tag{104}$$

with α the constant relative growth rate. This simple differential equation has the formula for **exponential growth** as its solution,

$$N(t) = A \exp \alpha t \tag{105}$$

A is sometimes replaced by $N(0)$. Not so long ago this model played a major part in the Report to the Club of Rome of Meadows *et al.* (1972), and it can be argued that it was already at the basis of Malthus' contention of 1740 that a human population, left to itself, would increase 'in geometric progression'. The exponential function was certainly known as a model of living populations to the formidable Belgian statistician of the early nineteenth century, Quetelet, well known for his interest in vital statistics. Quetelet was also aware of the drawback of the exponential function that indiscriminate extrapolation quickly leads to impossible values. He asked his pupil Verhulst, an artillery officer (like most practical mathematicians of his day) to think of something better, and Verhulst added an extra term to the differential equation (104), as in

$$\dot{N}(t) = \beta N(t)(W - N(t)) \tag{106}$$

where W denotes the upper limit or **saturation value** of N. If we express $N(t)$ as a fraction of W, say $Z(t) = N(t)/\mathrm{W}$, we have

$$\dot{Z}(t) = \beta Z(t)(1 - Z(t)) \tag{107}$$

The solution of this differential equation is of course the logistic function, as we know from (13), or

$$Z(t) = \exp(\alpha + \beta t)/(1 + \exp(\alpha + \beta t)) \tag{108}$$

Verhulst died soon afterwards, and his role was largely forgotten until Miner (1933) did him full justice nearly a century later. But the logistic growth curve survived. There are several processes where (107) is appropriate. Reed and Berkson (1929) mention examples from the literature of the nineteenth century where it is applied to autocatalytic chemical reactions, that is reactions which bring forth their own catalyst. This property accounts for the first term of (107), $\beta z(t)$, and the gradual exhaustion of the reagent accounts for the second.

Independently of this early work, the logistic was used in its original role as a model of human population growth by Pearl and Reed (1920). Pearl was a prodigious investigator of a wide variety of biological phenomena; in spite of his many other preoccupations, he went on in the next twenty years to apply the logistic growth curve to almost any living population from banana flies to the human population of the French colonies in North Africa — see Pearl (1927), and Pearl *et al.* (1928; 1940), for examples.

The basic idea that growth is proportional both to the level already attained and to the remaining room to the saturation ceiling is simple and effective, and the logistic model is used to this day to model population growth or, in market research, to describe the diffusion or market penetration of a new product or of new technologies. For new commodities that satisfy new needs like television, compact discs or video cameras, the growth of ownership is naturally proportional both to the penetration rate already achieved and to the size of the remaining potential market, and similar arguments apply to the diffusion of new products and techniques in industry. Note that the link with a process *over time* is essential for the derivation and the interpretation of these growth models.

The second source of the logit model is the statistical analysis of **bio-assay**, or the application of probability models to biological experiments, with the probit model of (41) with X in logarithms prominent. This model dates from the work of Bliss (1934) and Gaddum (1933), though Finney reports some extraordinary forerunners in his survey of the history; see Finney (1971, pp. 38–42).

The full flowering of this school probably coincides with the publication of the first edition of Finney's monograph in 1947. In the absence of electronic computing, estimation required various auxiliary tables, which were included as a matter of routine in textbooks and standard collections. At the same time Berkson, who had for some time been working on the subject with Reed (who had first used the logistic with Pearl for population forecasting) began to challenge the supremacy of the probit and to advocate the logit as a superior alternative; see Reed and Berkson (1929) and Berkson (1944; 1951; 1953). As Berkson excels in the clear and uncompromising statement of his views, much controversy ensued. The early economic applications of a bivariate probability model in the 1950s used the respectable probit model. Farrell (1954) used it to relate the ownership of motor cars of different vintage to household income, and Adam (1958) fitted lognormal demand curves to interview data of the willingness to buy indivisible items, such as cigarette lighters, at various prices. Aitchison and Brown's classic monograph about the lognormal distribution of 1957 illustrates that economists at that time did not take the logit model seriously, and followed the established preference of biologists for the probit model.

The first to generalise the logit model to more than two states, and to pass from the **bivariate** to the **multinomial** logit model was Theil (1969). This generalisation opens up a very wide field indeed. The lead in exploiting its possibilities now passed firmly to a group of American economists and students of traffic problems under the leadership of McFadden. The multinomial logit model was extensively applied to empirical studies of the choice of traffic mode, or **modal split**, and many theoretical problems were solved in the course of this applied work. McFadden and his collaborators generalised the logit model in several directions, and made it academically respectable by providing a theoretical framework in the **utility theory of discrete choice**. This links the logit model directly with the abstract mathematical theory of economic choice; on a more practical level, it greatly facilitates the discussion and interpretation of the model and of the estimated coefficients in terms that should appeal to economists. We shall deal at greater length with these matters in Chapters 3 and 4.

The survey article by Amemiya (1981) and the book of Maddala (1983) finally gave the multinomial logit model the status of a familiar research tool of empirical economic research, and this is the way we treat it in this introductory monograph.

3
The Multinomial Logit Model

3.1 The multinomial logit model

The multinomial model extends the logit to more than two states, and it is also the chosen vehicle for two other developments. The first is the theory of discrete choice, which provides a new justification and interpretation of the model, and the second is a generalisation of the model's parametrisation. Both elements could have been introduced in the bivariate model, for they apply perforce to this special case; but they gain their full flavour in the multinomial context.

The present chapter is hybrid. It does deal with the theory of discrete choice and with the wider parametrisation, but when it comes to implementation and estimation it is restricted to the **standard** multinomial model which is the nearest neighbour to the bivariate model of Chapter 2.

Multinomial probability models apply to any number of distinct states. Instead of the simple (0,1) dichotomy there are S possible states with index $s = 1, 2, \ldots, S$. These states are disjunct and exhaustive, i.e., they cover all possibilities, if necessary by the introduction of a residual category. In the analysis of private car ownership which concludes this chapter we consider four household car ownership categories, viz.

- household has no car;
- household has one new car;
- household has one used car;
- household has more than one car.

This classification could be extended by further distinguishing age or price classes of cars. Again, households can be classified by their housing status as

- house owners;
- rent payers;
- otherwise accommodated.

When we consider the choice of a mode of transport, or **modal split**, each trip may be made by

- walking;
- bicycle;
- own motor transport;
- public transport,

and so on. In spite of what the first example suggests there is no need for a natural ordering of the S states from 'less' to 'more', and if there is such an order it is not taken into account in the model. Multinomial probability models treat all states on the same footing, and are impervious to changes in their order. For **ordered response models**, which do respect (and require) a definite order, see Maddala (1983, p. 46) and the literature there cited.

As before, we consider individual observations (households, individuals, or trips), as realisations of experiments which carry the index i. A **multinomial probability model** then assigns probabilities P_{is} to the events 'case i is in state s', and these probabilities are determined by k characteristic attributes of i that are arranged in the vector $\mathbf{x}_i$. To record such events we define a random vector $\mathbf{y}_i$ of S elements with a single nonzero element equal to one, and a similar vector ι_s that has one in the sth place and zeros everywhere else. The event 'case i yields state s' is then denoted as

$$\mathbf{y}_i = \iota_s \tag{1}$$

with probability

$$P_{is} = Pr(\mathbf{y}_i = \iota_s) \qquad \text{for all } s = 1, 2, \ldots, S \tag{2}$$

A multinomial probability model defines these probabilities as functions of the $\mathbf{x}_i$ and of unknown parameters $\boldsymbol{\theta}$,

$$P_{is} = P_s(\mathbf{x}_i, \boldsymbol{\theta}) \tag{3}$$

For future reference we may arrange these probabilities in a vector of S elements, as in

$$\mathbf{p}_i = \mathbf{p}(\mathbf{x}_i, \boldsymbol{\theta}) \tag{4}$$

Obviously we require that

$$P_s(\mathbf{x}, \boldsymbol{\theta}) \geqslant 0 \tag{5}$$

$$\sum_s P_s(\mathbf{x}, \boldsymbol{\theta}) = 1 \tag{6}$$

for all conceivable $\mathbf{x}$ and all admissible $\boldsymbol{\theta}$—in fact, these conditions define what $\boldsymbol{\theta}$ are admissible. In the **standard multinomial logit model**, the probability function (3) is

$$P_s(\mathbf{x}_i, \boldsymbol{\theta}) = \exp(\mathbf{x}_i^{\mathrm{T}} \boldsymbol{\gamma}_s) / \sum_t \exp(\mathbf{x}_i^{\mathrm{T}} \boldsymbol{\gamma}_t) \tag{7}$$

The vector $\mathbf{x}_i$ of k characteristic attributes of the ith experiment or observation generally includes a dummy constant. The S $(k \times 1)$ vectors $\boldsymbol{\gamma}_s$ are the parameters of the model, symbolically lumped together into $\boldsymbol{\theta}$.

Clearly, the representation of the model in (7) has too many parameters: the vectors $\boldsymbol{\gamma}_s$ are determinate only up to an additive constant, for we may add $\boldsymbol{\alpha}$ to each $\boldsymbol{\gamma}_s$ without affecting the P_{is}. It follows that only the differences $(\boldsymbol{\gamma}_s - \boldsymbol{\gamma}_t)$ are determinate, and that for practical purposes one vector of k parameters is redundant: when it comes to estimation, or to inference about the parameters from the probabilities, the parameters of (7) are *not identified*. The remedy is to delete one set of k parameters by subtracting $\boldsymbol{\gamma}_1$ from all $\boldsymbol{\gamma}_s$, reducing $\boldsymbol{\gamma}_1$ to $\mathbf{0}$. Since we may (re)order the states at will it does not matter what state is taken as this **reference state** $s = 1$. To avoid confusion we define

$$\boldsymbol{\beta}_s = \boldsymbol{\gamma}_s - \boldsymbol{\gamma}_1 \tag{8}$$

(which implies $\boldsymbol{\beta}_1 = \mathbf{0}$), and rewrite (7) as

$$P_s(\mathbf{x}_i, \boldsymbol{\theta}) = \exp(\mathbf{x}_i^{\mathrm{T}}\boldsymbol{\beta}_s)/(1 + \sum_t \exp(\mathbf{x}_i^{\mathrm{T}}\boldsymbol{\beta}_t)) \qquad \text{for } s \neq 1 \tag{9a}$$

$$P_1(\mathbf{x}_i, \boldsymbol{\theta}) = 1/(1 + \sum_t \exp(\mathbf{x}_i^{\mathrm{T}}\boldsymbol{\beta}_t)) \tag{9b}$$

For $S = 2$ this reduces at once to the bivariate model of (2.6) and (2.18).

Equations (7) or (8) and (9) are equivalent representations of the standard multinomial logit model. We shall be using (7), with its nice symmetry in the S states, in theoretical discussions of the model, but (9) when it comes to estimation and practical implementation.

We have here presented the standard multinomial logit as a straightforward generalization of the bivariate logit, in the same vein as Theil (1969); but it can equally well be regarded as a special case of a much more general model. This is the **general logit model**

$$P_{is} = \exp(V_{is})/\sum_{t \in S_i} \exp(V_{it}), \qquad s \in S_i \tag{10}$$

The V_{is} are characteristics of the combination (i, s); at a later stage they can be specified as a particular function of the observable characteristics of the experiment $\mathbf{x}_i$ or $\mathbf{x}_{is}$ and of unknown parameters $\boldsymbol{\gamma}$ or $\boldsymbol{\gamma}_s$. Note that the summation now takes place over *sets* S_i of feasible or accessible states at experiment i, and that these sets may vary from one i to another. In an analysis of transport mode it will be found that some households have no car at their disposal, and others live in areas where there is no public transport; the actual choice of each household is therefore restricted to a specific subset from the wider set of all modes of transport.* Hence the need for varying sets S_i. We use the same symbol S_i or S for a set and for the number of elements in that set, without fear of confusion.

We refer to (10) as the **general logit model**; it is sometimes known, on account of its origin, as the **discrete choice model**. We discuss this background at some length in Section 3.3. Examples and applications in the later sections are however limited to the standard model, and other specifications are only considered in Chapter 4.

As before, we shall use a special notation for the logit probability, writing

$$Pl_s(Z) = Pl(Z_s) = \exp Z_s/\sum_t \exp Z_t \tag{11}$$

* In the extreme case, a household has a single option, and no choice; but probability models do not apply to that case.

The standard model (7) corresponds to

$$P_{is} = Pl(\mathbf{x}_i^{\mathrm{T}}\boldsymbol{\gamma}_s), \qquad S_i = S \text{ for all } i, \tag{12}$$

and (9) corresponds to

$$P_{is} = Pl(\mathbf{x}_i^{\mathrm{T}}\boldsymbol{\beta}_s), \qquad S_i = S \text{ for all } i, \quad \boldsymbol{\beta}_1 = \mathbf{0}, \tag{13}$$

and (10) to

$$P_{is} = Pl(V_{is}) \tag{14}$$

To show the relation of the standard model to the general model, compare (7) and (10) or (12) and (14). Both have the same logit form, which ensures that all probabilities are nonnegative and that they sum to one. In the standard model, V_{is} is a linear combination of observables and parameters, but this is no severe constraint. The two major restrictions are (1) the assumption of a single identical set of states $s = 1, 2, \ldots, S$ for all i, and (2) the particular repartition of observable characteristics and parameters in the specification of V_{is} as

$$V_{is} = \mathbf{x}_i^{\mathrm{T}}\boldsymbol{\gamma}_s \tag{15}$$

Note that the need to normalise the parameters by (8) is directly due to this particular form.

3.2 Properties of the model

To bring out the properties of the standard multinomial logit model we consider (7), with all S states treated in perfect symmetry; the corresponding properties of the common form (9) follow immediately upon the substitution of (8). We follow the same order as in Section 2.2.

To begin with, the multinomial logit does *not* share the monotonic behaviour of the bivariate logit probability. The derivative in respect of the jth element of $\mathbf{x}$ is

$$\partial Pl_s/\partial X_j = Pl_s(\gamma_{sj} - \sum_t \gamma_{tj} Pl_t) \tag{16}$$

By the values of the Pl_s and Pl_t, this depends on the point of evaluation, as in the bivariate case; but now it can also vary in sign according to the value of $\mathbf{x}$ and of the concomitant probabilities. Any logit probability may thus exhibit non-monotonic behaviour with respect to $\mathbf{x}^{\mathrm{T}}\boldsymbol{\beta}_s$; we shall come across an example in Fig. 3.2 in Section 3.6, with the probability first increasing and then declining as one element of $\mathbf{x}$ varies over its entire range. It also follows that the sign of $\beta_{sj} = (\gamma_{sj} - \gamma_{1j})$ does not indicate in what sense Pl_s will vary with an increase in X_j.

As before, the derivatives can be turned into quasi-elasticities

$$\eta_{sj} = X_j \partial Pl_s/\partial X_j = Pl_s X_j(\gamma_{sj} - \sum_t \gamma_{tj} Pl_t) \tag{17}$$

which indicate the percentage point change in Pl_s upon a one percent increase in X_j. These measures satisfy

$$\sum_s \eta_{sj} = 0 \tag{18}$$

Quasi-elasticities are still superior to the $\boldsymbol{\gamma}$ coefficients and to derivatives and elasticities by their ease of interpretation, but we must be aware that like the derivatives they, too, may change in sign as well as in value when they are evaluated at different points.

The analogue to the **log odds ratio** of (2.11) for the probabilities of any pair of states (s, t) is

$$R(s, t) = \log(P_s/P_t) \tag{19}$$

where we have omitted the common argument $\mathbf{x}$. For the standard multinomial logit we have, by (7),

$$R(s, t) = \mathbf{x}^{\mathrm{T}}(\gamma_s - \gamma_t) \tag{20}$$

The general logit model (10) yields a similar expression for any pair (s, t) that belongs to the choice set S_i

$$R_i(s, t) = V_{is} - V_{it} \tag{21}$$

The remarkable fact is that in both cases $R_i(s, t)$ depends exclusively on characteristics of the two states concerned, and that it is independent of the number and the nature of all other states that are simultaneously considered. The odds ratio is therefore not affected by the addition or deletion of an element of this set. This property, which is known as **independence from irrelevant alternatives** (IIA), can easily lead to inacceptable results since it also applies to highly relevant alternatives. The standard example is that of the red and blue buses.* Consider the choice among several modes of transport, with s denoting some form of private transport like driving or cycling, and t public transport or, specifically, travel by a red bus, in a situation where no other public transport is available. Assume now that a new bus service is introduced that is almost identical to the existing bus but uses blue buses. The model (10) holds as before, but the choice set is enlarged by the new option. According to (20), the log odds ratio for (t, s) and indeed all odds ratios from the original choice set are unchanged, so that the new bus service is supposed to gain its share of the market by a proportional reduction of the probabilities of all existing transport modes. This is an unpalatable result. It stands to reason that red bus traffic is much more affected by the introduction of the blue bus than the other travel modes, and this should be reflected in the values of the $R(s, t)$. But in the general logit model (and in all its special forms) this is not the case.

* This often quoted example is attributed to McFadden, but I have not been able to find the original reference in print. Debreu (1960) demonstrated the IIA by contrasting several recordings of the same concerto with a live performance.

The IIA property is due to the blind indifference of the model to any similarity or dissimilarity of the S states, which are all treated on the same footing. This is a substantive assumption, and in many applications it is clearly inappropriate. The defect can not be remedied by an adjustment of the general logit model, but only by passing to a different probability model like the multinomial probit of Section 3.4 or the nested logit model of Section 4.4.

We note in passing that the symmetrical treatment of all states (and the IIA property in particular) may have some bearing on the definition of what constitutes a distinct state. This definition is not self-evident. In many analyses the classification of the alternatives that form the choice set is constructed by adding together items from a much more detailed enumeration in the primary data set. Such early stages of planning or preparing an empirical analysis are seldom fully discussed. The terms of classification are of course largely established by the practical purpose of the study, or the policy issues at hand. Clearly, however, the analyst should also bear in mind what properties the model imposes on the distinct states concerned.

3.3 Discrete choice theory

Some of the justificatory arguments for the bivariate model of Section 2.2 carry over, with minor adjustments, to the multinomial case. To begin with, we may again invoke the expedience of several obvious approximations. Thus if we expect the probabilities P_{is} to depend on regressor variables $\mathbf{x}_i$, it is common practice to express their effect in a linear combination $\mathbf{x}_i^{\mathrm{T}}\gamma_s$; the exponential transformation turns this into a nonnegative quantity; and

$$P_{is} = \exp(\mathbf{x}_i^{\mathrm{T}}\gamma_s)/\sum_t \exp(\mathbf{x}_i^{\mathrm{T}}\gamma_t)$$

serves to respect the condition (6) in a symmetrical fashion. The standard multinomial logit (7) is thus derived in three easy steps. This is a shallow but effective and robust argument.

While the expected duration argument of (2.20) likewise at once carries over to the multinomial case, the random element models of Sections 2.2 and 2.3 are not so easily amended to yield a multinomial logit; a justification along these lines is provided instead by the much deeper and by now classical derivation of the general model (10) from **discrete choice theory**. This wider paradigm first arose in mathematical psychology, where the need to explain variations in repeated experimental measurements of individual preferences led to the notion of **probabilistic choice**. The seminal work is that of Thurstone (1927), and some ideas can even be traced back all the way to Fechner (1860).

In the 1950s, theorists turned to the abstract mathematical representation of the choice process by the choice probabilities P_s of a given subject.* This leads to a probabilistic analogue of the preference relations of the classical theory of

* For a survey of the work in this field, see Luce and Suppes (1965).

consumer behaviour. The deterministic relation 's is preferred to t' is for instance replaced by 'given the choice between s and t, the probability that s is selected exceeds 0.5'. The next step is to search for equivalents of properties like the transitivity of preference relations, and to see whether probabilities with the requisite regularity properties can be linked to an underlying utility function. At this stage, one may choose between a **random utility model**, where the actual choice reflects the maximisation of random utility indicators of the feasible options, and a **constant utility model**, where the utilities are determinate but the choice process is probabilistic. In the latter context, Luce (1959) imposes the **choice axiom**, whereby the conditional probability of selecting the state s out of a given subset is constant, regardless of the wider choice set to which this subset belongs. This axiom is needed to ensure that the probabilistic preference relation between two states holds whatever other states are considered; once it has been adopted, the theory can be developed further without the limitation to a fixed and fully enumerated choice set, which may raise awkward problems. Luce also shows that the choice axiom implies the existence of a function ϕ_s such that

$$\Pr\,(s \text{ is chosen out of } S) = \phi_s / \sum_{t \in S} \phi_t \qquad (22)$$

where S is *any* set that contains s and at least one other choice; for the time being, we omit the index i of the conditions surrounding the choice process. This is called a **strict utility model**. With minor additional assumptions, Luce (1959) proceeds to derive (10) from (22).

We here note that in constant utility models, the choice axiom by (22) implies the IIA property of the ensuing probability model. As we have argued above, the question whether this property is acceptable or not is a matter of judgement about the need for an asymmetrical treatment of the various states, e.g. in view of their degrees of similarity or dissimilarity. Thus the choice axiom is not just a technical device for excluding some difficult cases, but a substantive assumption that imposes a certain structure on the choice set and on the definition of what constitutes a separate choice.

We prefer to derive (10) from a **random utility** model since this is more in keeping with the arguments of Section 2.3. In this approach the choice reflects the maximisation of (perceived) utility, which is a random attribute of feasible choices. The utility of choice s (always under the given conditions of experiment or observation i, omitted from the notation) is defined as

$$U_s = V_s + \varepsilon_s \qquad (23)$$

where V_s is a systematic component and ε_s is a random disturbance. Manski (1977) lists the reasons for this random component: it reflects unobserved characteristics of the ith experimental situation, unobserved taste variation, and similar imperfections which force the analyst to treat the choice process as random. It may also accommodate a genuine indeterminacy of individual behaviour which calls for a probabilistic description, although strictly this view is alien to deterministic utility maximisation over random utilities.

With random utilities U_s and a feasible choice set S, utility maximisation implies

$$P_s = \Pr(U_s > U_t \text{ for all } t \neq s \text{ in } S) \tag{24}$$

This determines P_s once the stochastic specification of the random elements ε_s of (23) is given. It has been established by McFadden that P_s is given by the general multinomial logit model (10) if the disturbances ε_s are independently and identically distributed by a type I extreme value distribution of standard form. To show this, we follow the derivation of McFadden (1974) and Domencich and McFadden (1975).

First, we rewrite (24) as

$$P_s = \Pr(U_s > \tilde{U}^s) \tag{25}$$

with

$$\tilde{U}^s = \max(U_t, t \in \bar{S}) \tag{26a}$$

$$\bar{S} = S - s \tag{26b}$$

In words, U_s must exceed $\tilde{U}^s$, which is the largest of all other utilities.* Now consider the distribution function of U_s or

$$F_{s1}(x) = \Pr(U_s \leqslant x) \tag{27}$$

For $\tilde{U}^s$ we have of course

$$F_{s2}(x) = Pr(\tilde{U}^s \leqslant x) = \Pr(U_t \leqslant x, U_v \leqslant x, U_w \leqslant x, \ldots) \tag{28}$$

Since the ε_s are stochastically independent, so are the U_s (although they are not identically distributed, having different parameters V_s). As a result

$$F_{s2}(x) = \prod_{t \in \bar{S}} F_{t1}(x) \tag{29}$$

Given proper analytical expressions for F_{s1} and F_{s2}, the probability (25) can be evaluated by the convolution theorem.† By this theorem we have for any two independent random variables y and z

$$\Pr(y > z) = \int_{-\infty}^{+\infty} F'_y(t) F_z(t)\, \mathrm{d}t \tag{30}$$

Hence

$$\Pr(U_s > \tilde{U}^s) = \int_{-\infty}^{+\infty} F'_1(t) F_2(t)\, \mathrm{d}t \tag{31}$$

This completes the preliminaries.

* We ignore the possibility of a tie which would arise if U_s were equal to $\tilde{U}^s$. In the algebra that follows, strict and weak inequalities are treated in similar cavalier fashion.

† For the convolution theorem, see Mood *et al.* (1974), p. 186.

We now assume that the disturbances ε_s are independent and identically distributed according to a **type I extreme value distribution in standard form**, sometimes also called a **Weibull** or **Gumbel** distribution. This is the distribution with distribution function

$$F(x) = \exp(-\exp(-x)). \tag{32}$$

It follows by (23) that

$$F_{s1}(x) = \Pr(U_s \leqslant x) = \Pr(\varepsilon_s \leqslant x - V_s) \tag{33}$$

so that

$$F_{s1}(x) = \exp(-\exp(V_s - x)) \tag{34}$$

is the distribution function of U_s. By (29) we then have

$$\begin{aligned} F_{s2}(x) &= \exp(-\sum_{t \in S} \exp(V_t - x)) \\ &= \exp(-\exp(\tilde{V}_s - x)) \end{aligned} \tag{35a}$$

with

$$\tilde{V}_s = -\log \sum_{t \in \tilde{S}} \exp V_t \tag{35b}$$

Upon inserting these expressions into (31) and hence into (25), we obtain

$$\begin{aligned} P_s &= \int_{-\infty}^{\infty} \exp(V_s - t) . \exp(-\exp(V_s - t)) . \exp(-\exp(\tilde{V}_s - t)) \, \mathrm{d}t \\ &= \exp V_s \int_{-\infty}^{\infty} \exp -t . \exp\{-\exp - t . (\exp V_s + \exp \tilde{V}_s)\} \, \mathrm{d}t \end{aligned} \tag{36}$$

We make use of

$$\mathrm{d}/\mathrm{d}t \exp(-A \exp -t) = A \exp -t . \exp(-A \exp -t)) \tag{37a}$$

with

$$A = \exp V_s + \exp \tilde{V}_s \tag{36b}$$

to write

$$P_s = \exp V_s / (\exp V_s + \exp \tilde{V}_s) . \int_{-\infty}^{+\infty} \mathrm{d} \exp(-\exp -t A) \tag{38}$$

and obtain

$$P_s = \exp V_s / (\exp V_s + \exp \tilde{V}_s) \tag{39}$$

Finally we use (35b) to find the expression we are looking for, namely

$$P_s = \exp V_s / \sum_t \exp V_t \tag{40}$$

This completes the derivation of the general logit model (10) from random utility considerations. Note that the **bivariate** logit model of Section 2.1 follows from first principles in the same way if we put V_s equal to V_1 and V_t equal to V_0, with 1 and 0 denoting the two states.

The crucial analytical assumption in the above argument is of course that the ε_s are independent and identically distributed according to the standard type I distribution (32). This is a somewhat contrived assumption, adopted mainly because it leads to the desired result. What does it entail? The general form of the type I extreme value distribution function is

$$F(x) = \exp(-\exp(-(x-\mu)/\lambda)), \tag{41}$$

and the **standard form** has zero for the location parameter μ and unit for the scale parameter λ. Johnson and Kotz (1970: I, pp. 272–89) give a survey of this distribution and its properties. There is no clear link of the present usage of the distribution with its derivation from the asymptotic behaviour of extreme sample values. As for the use of the standard form, for z distributed according to (41) we find

$$Ez = \mu + 0.57722\lambda \tag{42}$$

$$\operatorname{var} z = 1.64493\lambda^2 \tag{43}$$

In the standard form of the distribution, μ is zero and λ is 1; hence the disturbances ε_s have a common mean of .57 and a common standard deviation of 1.28. Their probability density function is shown in Figure 3.1. It is not so very different from a Normal distribution with the same mean and variance.

Whether the assumption of a common mean and variance for all ε_s is an

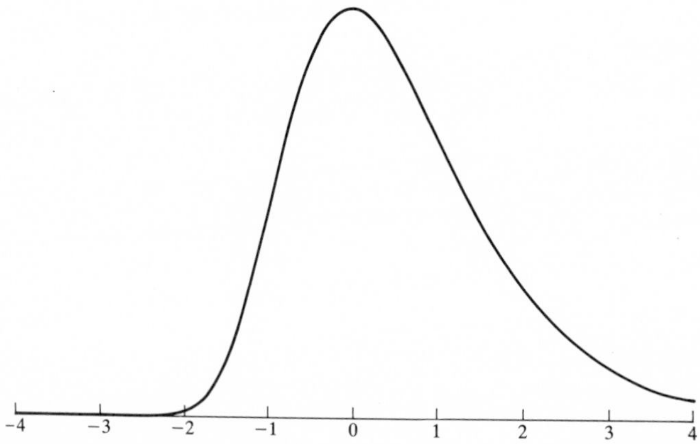

Fig. 3.1 Extreme value probability density function in standard form.

effective restriction depends on the specification of V_s. If we allow for distinct parameters μ_s and λ_s for each s the argument of (34) is changed to

$$V_s^* = (V_s + \mu_s)/\lambda_s. \tag{44}$$

The specification of V_s for the standard multinomial logit is of course

$$V_{si} = \mathbf{x}_i^{\mathrm{T}} \gamma_s \tag{45}$$

with a constant 1 among the elements of **x**, i.e. an intercept in the expression. In this case the parameters μ_s and λ_s cannot be identified, as they are absorbed into the elements of γ_s; the common values imposed by the standard distribution are therefore quite innocuous. Moreover the addition of 0.577 to all intercepts γ_{0s} is undone when we pass to the β_{0s} of (8). But with other specifications of V_{si} the issue is not so easily resolved.

So much for the algebra and for some carping about the implicit assumptions of the model. This operational discrete choice theory has been developed in the 1970s by McFadden and his school in close connection with applied research serving policy analyses of transport and travel demand. It has proved a quite powerful paradigm. The least one can say is that it permits the interpretation of the systematic terms V_s as if they reflect the utility of one option relative to the others. In the view of its adherents, it is also superior to other derivations of the logit formula in that it permits a **structural analysis** of observed discrete choice in the sense that the probability model is directly linked to underlying maximising behaviour. Forceful statements of this doctrine can be found in the work of McFadden, like his early review article (1976), in Manski's writings (1977), in the textbook of Ben-Akiva and Lerman (1987), and in the collection of advanced papers of Manski and McFadden (1977a). Discrete choice theory does indeed at first sight provide an instance of that rare and much sought after phenomenon, economic theory dictating the form of an empirically valid mathematical function; but in order to make the theory work, some arbitrary underlying assumptions are technically necessary, as we have seen. It is a greater achievement of the theory that it has proved an effective vehicle for the introduction of new extensions and generalisations. The utility foundation is essential for the **conditional logit model**, and a generalisation of the extreme value distribution has yielded the **nested logit**, that is free from the IIA property. We return to these models in Chapter 4.

3.4 The multinomial probit model

The binomial probit model of Section 2.3 can be generalised to more than two states in the same way as the logit model. As above, we assume utility maximisation over S random utilities of the form (23)

$$U_s = V_s + \varepsilon_s$$

which leads to (24),

$$P_s = Pr(U_s > U_t \text{ for all } t \neq s)$$

If the joint density of the S U_s is $f(.)$, the probability (say) P_1 is given by the multiple integral

$$P_1 = \int_{-\infty}^{\infty} \int_{-\infty}^{U_1} \int_{-\infty}^{U_1} \cdots \int_{-\infty}^{U_1} f(U_1, U_2, \ldots U_S) \mathrm{d}U_1 \mathrm{d}U_2 \cdots \mathrm{d}U_S \qquad (46)$$

But for the systematic term V_s, the distribution of the U_s is determined by the distribution of the ε_s, and this is a matter of assumptions. If the ε_s are independent and identically distributed with a standard type I extreme value distribution, P_s is given by the logit function $Pl(V_s)$, as has been demonstrated in the preceding section. But if the ε_s have a standardized joint Normal distribution, as in the probit model, (46) does not permit of an analytical solution, and the integral must be evaluated by numerical methods. This also holds for the bivariate probit model of eq. (2.41) (although we could have recourse to standard statistical tables), but the complexity and the extent of the computations increase rapidly as the number of dimensions increases. Note that in maximum likelihood estimation the probability (46) must be evaluated for all observations at each iteration. The need for these laborious calculations is a major drawback of the multinomial probit, and has restricted its applications.

Just as in the multinomial logit model, the distribution of the random disturbances is standardised with respect to their means and variances, if only to permit identification of the parameters of the V_s. But in contrast to the logit model their stochastic independence is a special case: the joint Normal distribution permits as a matter of course for a nondiagonal covariance matrix, and moreover this presents no great additional analytical difficulties. The advantage of the joint Normal over the extreme value distribution is thus that it allows naturally for correlations among the disturbances; such correlations can also be introduced among disturbances with an extreme value distribution (see the nested logit model of Section 4.4), but this is a far more difficult task. Since the condition (24) bears on a comparison among the S utilities, a correlation matrix of order $(S - 1)$ is sufficient to describe the joint distribution that determines P_s.

This generalisation is quite important. Once the disturbances, and hence the utilities, are no longer necessarily independent, the restrictive IIA property is no longer automatically imposed, but relegated to the position of a special case that may or may not obtain. With the additional correlation parameters, the multinomial probit is thus much more flexible than the logit models of the present chapter.

Hausman and Wise (1978) have made a thorough investigation of the empirical performance of the model in a case study with $S = 3$. A strong plea for the model can be found in the book by Daganzo (1979), and Amemiya (1985, p. 307–10) gives a survey of the debate. We do not pursue the subject here.

3.5 Estimation of multinomial probability models

In this section we apply the principles of maximum likelihood estimation of Section 2.4 to a general multinomial probability model, not necessarily of the logit type. We recall that we have n individual observations i and, in the general case, a set S_i of states s at each i. A corresponding set of S_i scalars y_{is} with a single element 1 for some s, say $s(i)$, and zeros elsewhere, records the observed states. These y_{is} may be arranged in a vector $\mathbf{y}_i$, as we did in (1), but note that the number of elements varies with i according to S_i.

We also have a probability model that specifies a corresponding vector $\mathbf{p}_i$ of probabilities, as in (4), with elements

$$P_{is} = P_{is}(\mathbf{x}_i, \boldsymbol{\theta})$$

for all $s \in S_i$, with $\mathbf{x}_i$ a vector of regressor variables and $\boldsymbol{\theta}$ a vector of say k parameters. Note that

$$\sum_{s \in S_i} P_{is} = 1 \tag{47}$$

and

$$Ey_{is} = P_{is}, \qquad E\mathbf{y}_i = \mathbf{P}_i \tag{48}$$

In the present case the maximum likelihood estimates are best calculated by the iterative scoring method of (2.60), or

$$\boldsymbol{\theta}_{t+1} = \boldsymbol{\theta}_t + \mathbf{H}(\boldsymbol{\theta}_t)^{-1}\mathbf{q}(\boldsymbol{\theta}_t) \tag{49}$$

For this scheme as well as for the asymptotic standard errors of the estimates and for some common tests we shall need (1) the loglikelihood function, (2) the score vector $\mathbf{q}$ of its first derivatives of (2.51), and (3) the information matrix $\mathbf{H}$ of (2.56). In this section we give an outline of these expressions for a probability model, but neither here nor in the sequel shall we spell out the full results for any particular model that will be considered; most expressions can be derived by the ground rules of differentiation. The actual calculations will moreover often be performed by a standard routine from a computer program package, or by a program that has been especially designed by the analyst. In both cases it is sufficient to indicate here in broad outline how the various expressions can be constructed and what properties they have.

As always we assume independence of the observations, so that the sample loglikelihood is simply the sum over i of the loglikelihoods of the single observations. Its first and second derivatives obey the same rule. We take some care only over the expressions for a single observation i.

The loglikelihood for observation i is

$$\log L_i = \sum_{s \in S_i} y_{is} \log P_{is} \tag{50}$$

Note that this sum over s actually consists of a single term, as there is only a single nonzero y_{is}. The sample loglikelihood is then

$$\log L = \sum_i \log L_i = \sum_i \sum_{s \in S_i} y_{is} \log P_{is} \tag{51}$$

For the score vector of first derivatives $\mathbf{q}$ we consider a typical element q_h, which is the derivative of $\log L$ in respect of the hth element of $\boldsymbol{\theta}$. For observation i this follows from (50) as

$$q_{ih} = \sum_{s \in S_i} \frac{y_{is}}{P_{is}} \cdot \frac{\partial P_{is}}{\partial \theta_h} \tag{52}$$

The summation over s again yields only a single term. For the entire sample we have

$$q_h = \sum_i \sum_{s \in S_i} \frac{y_{is}}{P_{is}} \cdot \frac{\partial P_{is}}{\partial \theta_h} \tag{53}$$

For a typical element of the Hessian matrix $\mathbf{Q}$ of second derivatives of the loglikelihood function, the contribution of observation i is

$$Q_{ihm} = \sum_{s \in S_i} \left\{ \frac{y_{is}}{P_{is}} \frac{\partial P_{is}}{\partial \theta_h \partial \theta_m} - \frac{y_{is}}{P_{is}^2} \cdot \frac{\partial P_{is}}{\partial \theta_h} \cdot \frac{\partial P_{is}}{\partial \theta_m} \right\} \tag{54}$$

The summation over s once more yields only a single term. For the information matrix we reverse the sign and take the expected value by substituting the expectations of the y_{is} of (48). With Ey_{is} instead of y_{is}, the summation is no longer trivial. Since $Ey_{is} = P_{is}$, the first term of (54) turns into a sum of second derivatives, which vanishes since the P_{is} sum to 1 by (47), and the second term is simplified. The result is

$$H_{ihm} = \sum_{s \in S_i} \frac{1}{P_{is}} \cdot \frac{\partial P_{is}}{\partial \theta_n} \cdot \frac{\partial P_{is}}{\partial \theta_m} \tag{55}$$

The value for the entire sample is of course

$$H_{hm} = \sum_i \sum_{s \in S_i} \frac{1}{P_{is}} \cdot \frac{\partial P_{is}}{\partial \theta_n} \cdot \frac{\partial P_{is}}{\partial \theta_m} \tag{56}$$

If we arrange the derivatives of the P_{si} in respect of the k elements of $\boldsymbol{\theta}$ in a $(S_i \times k)$ matrix $\mathbf{A}$ and define $\tilde{\mathbf{p}}_i$ as a diagonal matrix with the P_{si} as its elements, the information matrix $\mathbf{H}_i$ of (55) can be rewritten as

$$\mathbf{H}_i = \mathbf{A}_i^{\mathrm{T}} \tilde{\mathbf{p}}_i^{-1} \mathbf{A}_i \tag{57}$$

Pre- and postmultiplication of this expression by a nondegenerate vector z yields a weighted sum of squares, with positive weights, so that $\mathbf{H}_i$ is a positive semidefinite matrix for any feasible set of parameter values, provided k exceeds S_i: we must have at least one parameter for each state. But then $\mathbf{H}$ of (56) is also positive semidefinite for all parameter values. If we disregard the possibility that $\mathbf{H}$ is singular, this means that the scoring algorithm (49) will always converge to a maximum, whatever the starting values. The argument moreover suggests (but does not prove) that the Hessian is negative definite for all parameter vectors, so that the loglikelihood function is everywhere convex and has a single unique maximum.* Note that this argument holds for any multinomial probability model: for all varieties of the logit model, for the probit model, and for any other probability model that may be devised.

In the sequel, when it comes to the estimation of specific models, we need now only specify the probabilities P_{is} and their derivatives in respect of the elements of $\boldsymbol{\theta}$ to obtain the loglikelihood (50), the score vector (52) and the information matrix (55) for a single observation, and these can then be summed to give the elements for the scoring algorithm (49).

3.6 Estimation of the standard model

We now apply the principles of estimation of the last section to the standard multinomial logit model (9), or

$$Pl_{is} = \exp(\mathbf{x}_i^{\mathrm{T}}\boldsymbol{\beta}_s)\Big/\left(1 + \sum_{t=2}^{S} \exp(\mathbf{x}_i^{\mathrm{T}}\boldsymbol{\beta}_t)\right) \tag{58a}$$

$$Pl_{i1} = 1\Big/\left(1 + \sum_{t=2}^{S} \exp(\mathbf{x}_i^{\mathrm{T}}\boldsymbol{\beta}_s)\right) \tag{58b}$$

With S states and k elements in the regressor vector $\mathbf{x}$ (including a dummy constant 1) there are $(S-1) \times k$ parameters to be estimated, and the parameter vector $\boldsymbol{\beta}$ consists of $(S-1)$ subvectors $\boldsymbol{\beta}_s$ for $s = 2, 3, \ldots, S$, each of length k.

No problems arise in the substitution of (58) into the log likelihood (51). For the elements of $\mathbf{q}_i$ of (53), however, some further algebra is in order. To begin with we must distinguish between the derivatives of Pl_{is} in respect of the elements of its 'own' parameter vector $\boldsymbol{\beta}_s$ and the derivatives in respect of the members of alien subsets $\boldsymbol{\beta}_t$ with $t \neq s$. From (58) we find

$$\partial Pl_{is}/\partial \beta_h = X_{hi} Pl_{is}(1 - Pl_{is}) \qquad \text{if } \beta_h \in \boldsymbol{\beta}_s \tag{59a}$$

$$\partial Pl_{is}/\partial \beta_h = -X_{hi} Pl_{is} Pl_{it} \qquad \text{if } \beta_h \in \boldsymbol{\beta}_t, \quad t \neq s \tag{50b}$$

With $s = 1$ the second expression applies to Pl_{i1}, too. We substitute these expressions into (52), with $\boldsymbol{\beta}_r$ denoting the parameter subvector to which β_h

* See Cramer (1986a, pp. 75–6, 154) for a further discussion. McFadden (1974, p. 119) has listed the conditions for the Hessian of the logit model to be everywhere negative definite.

actually belongs. This gives

$$q_{ih} = \frac{y_{is}}{P_{is}} X_{hi} Pl_{ir}(1 - Pl_{ir}) - \sum_{s \neq r} \frac{y_{is}}{P_{is}} X_{hi} Pl_{is} Pl_{ir}$$

$$= X_{hi}(y_{ir} - Pl_{ir} y_{ir} - Pl_{ir} \sum_{s \neq r} y_{is}$$

$$= X_{hi}(y_{ir} - Pl_{ir}) \tag{60}$$

where we make use of the fact that by their definition the y_{is} sum to 1. For the entire rth segment of $\mathbf{q}_i$, corresponding to $\boldsymbol{\beta}_r$, we have

$$\mathbf{q}_{ir} = (y_{ir} - Pl_{ir})\mathbf{x}_i \tag{61}$$

or, for the whole sample,

$$\mathbf{q}_r = \sum_i (y_{ir} - Pl_{ir})\, \mathbf{x}_i \tag{62}$$

Note that in the summation in the right-hand side of (62) over i many y_{ir} will be zero, and only a limited number will be 1, namely the observations with state r.

Both (61) and (62) denote vectors of length k (since $\mathbf{x}_i$ is such a vector), as they should, and there are $(S - 1)$ of them for $r = 2, 3, \ldots, S$. Placed one under the other they form the column vector $\mathbf{q}$.

It can be seen from (62) that the random variables y_{ir} disappear upon further differentiation of $\mathbf{q}$ in respect of elements of $\boldsymbol{\beta}$. For the present model, the Hessian matrix of second derivatives $\mathbf{Q}$ is therefore nonrandom, and for the information matrix $\mathbf{H}$, defined earlier in (2.56) as

$$\mathbf{H} = -E\mathbf{Q}$$

we need only reverse the sign of $\mathbf{Q}$. While $\mathbf{H}$ is easily obtained in this manner, we shall here find it by substituting the derivatives of (59) into (55), which gives a typical (h, m)th element of $\mathbf{H}_i$, and hence of $\mathbf{H}$. As before, we must distinguish between the case that β_h and β_m both belong to the same subvector $\boldsymbol{\beta}_r$, say, and the case that one belongs to $\boldsymbol{\beta}_r$ and the other to $\boldsymbol{\beta}_t$. The matrix $\mathbf{H}$ is of the order $k \times (S - 1)$, and it can be partitioned into $(S - 1) \times (S - 1)$ submatrices of order $k \times k$, say $\mathbf{H}_{(s,t)}$. The $\mathbf{H}_{(r,r)}$ lie on the main diagonal and the $\mathbf{H}_{(r,t)}$ are the off-diagonal blocks.

We first take the case that both β_h and β_m belong to the same subvector β_r. Straightforward substitution of (59) into (55) gives

$$H_{ihm} = \frac{1}{P_{ir}} X_{hi} X_{mi} (Pl_{ir}(1 - Pl_{ir})^2 + \sum_{s \neq r} \frac{1}{P_{is}} X_{hi} X_{mi} (Pl_{is} Pl_{ir})^2$$

$$= X_{hi} X_{mi} \left\{ Pl_{ir}(1 - Pl_{ir})^2 + \sum_{s \neq r} Pl_{is} Pl_{ir}^2 \right\}$$

$$= X_{hi} X_{mi} Pl_{ir}(1 - Pl_{ir}) \tag{63}$$

In the passage from the second to the third line we make use of the summation of the Pl_{is} over all s to 1. If β_h and β_m belong to different subvectors $\boldsymbol{\beta}_r$ and $\boldsymbol{\beta}_t$, we obtain by a similar but slightly lengthier development

$$H_{ihm} = -X_{hi}X_{mi}Pl_{ir}Pl_{it} \tag{64}$$

The diagonal submatrices of $\mathbf{H}_i$ are obtained from (63), and the others from (64); we find

$$\mathbf{H}_{(rr)i} = Pl_{ir}(1 - Pl_{ir})\mathbf{x}_i\mathbf{x}_i^{\mathrm{T}} \tag{65a}$$

$$\mathbf{H}_{(rt)i} = -Pl_{ir}Pl_{it}\mathbf{x}_i\mathbf{x}_i^{\mathrm{T}} \tag{65b}$$

The complete matrix $\mathbf{H}$ is obtained by summing these expressions over i and arranging the blocks as indicated.

All the elements needed for the estimation of the standard multinomial logit model have now been covered. For given parameter values $\boldsymbol{\beta}_0$ the probabilities P_{is} follow from (58); the loglikelihood can now be evaluated by using (51), and the current values of $\mathbf{q}$ and $\mathbf{H}$ can be constructed from (62) and (65). With these expressions, the iterative algorithm (49) can be applied to successive values of $\boldsymbol{\beta}$, once starting values have been provided and a convergence criterion has been set. The end result covers the same elements as in the bivariate case, viz. parameter estimates, their asymptotic variances, and the value of $\log L$ at its maximum. Other statistics, such as derivatives and (quasi-)elasticities, with their standard errors, can be derived as before. All the considerations about maximum likelihood estimation in general of Section 2.4 apply as a matter of course.

In practice, estimation is usually carried out by means of some standard program package. If a large number of logit analyses on a large scale (with many states and large data sets) is contemplated, it may however be worthwhile to construct an estimation program of one's own along the lines sketched above. Such a specific logit program is usually much faster than the logit option of a general estimation program package. But even if standard program are used, the above algebra may help to understand what is going on, and occasionally what is going wrong.

In this respect much of the discussion of the bivariate logit estimation at the end of Section 2.5 applies equally here. Upon carrying out the summation of (65), we again find that $\mathbf{H}$ closely resembles $\mathbf{X}^{\mathrm{T}}\mathbf{X}$, the regressor moment matrix from linear regression; the difference lies in a fairly complicated weighting scheme, with various products of the form $Pl_{ir}Pl_{it}$ forming the weights. It follows that the arguments about the structure of the regressor matrix $\mathbf{X}$ once more apply. It should have full rank, and preferably little collinearity in the interest of fairly precise parameter estimates, with small asymptotic variances; it should moreover be well balanced, in the sense that the diagonal elements of $\mathbf{X}^{\mathrm{T}}\mathbf{X}$ are of the same order of magnitude, to facilitate its numerical inversion.

Again, the estimated probabilities will once more on average reproduce the observed frequencies. The MLE of the parameters define ML predictions of the probabilities,

$$\hat{P}l_{is} = Pl(\mathbf{x}_i, \hat{\theta}) \tag{66}$$

and these must satisfy the first-order conditions for a maximum $\mathbf{q}_s = \mathbf{0}$, or, by (62),

$$\sum_i (y_{is} - \hat{P}l_{is})\mathbf{x}_i = \mathbf{0} \tag{67}$$

When we consider the dummy '1' variable among the $\mathbf{x}_i$, this simplifies to

$$\sum_i \hat{P}l_{is} = \sum_i y_{is} = n_s \tag{68}$$

with n_s denoting the number of observations with state s. Hence the mean predicted probability of a state equals its sample frequency. This also holds for the base-line estimate, when we reduce $\mathbf{x}_i^{\mathrm{T}}\boldsymbol{\beta}_s$ to a vector of constants, say $\boldsymbol{\beta}_0$. The probabilities $Pl^{\circ}(\hat{\boldsymbol{\beta}}_0)$ are constants, too, and it follows immediately from (68) that

$$\hat{P}l^{\circ} = n_s/n \tag{69}$$

The corresponding base-line loglikehood follows at once from (51) as

$$\log L^{\circ} = \sum_s n_s \log n_s - n \log n \tag{70}$$

This can be used in an overall LR test of the significance of all regressor variables (other than the intercept) for the S states of the multinomial logit, along the lines of (2.61).

If we consider only a limited number of regressor variables that are all measured in intervals or classes, the sample data consist of a cross-classification of all observations by these variables with the frequencies of all S states in each cell. This is the case of **grouped observations**. As in the bivariate case, treated at some length in Section 2.6, the estimation from such data presents no problems when we regard the grouped observations simply as repeated individual observations. It would be tedious to repeat the derivation of the expressions needed for estimation.

Some further techniques for dealing with grouped data from Section 2.6 do not apply equally easily. Minimum chi-square estimation is not practised for multinomial models, and the graphical inspection of grouped data in logit transformation as advocated in Section 2.7 is for obvious reasons not applicable to the multinomial case. We may however still apply something like the logit transformation of (2.92) to multinomial data. Let f_{js} denote the relative frequency of state s in cell j of some given (cross-)classification of the data, and f_{j0} the frequency of the reference state. When we equate frequencies to probabilities, the log odds ratio (19) of the standard multinomial logit satisfies

$$\log(f_{js}/f_{j0}) \approx \mathbf{x}_j^{\mathrm{T}}\boldsymbol{\beta}_s \tag{71}$$

This again suggests the use of linear regression estimation. The comments (and strictures) of Section 2.6 apply. Note that transformations like (71) have become quite common in regression analyses of various **shares** that have little or nothing to do with choice frequencies apart from the fact that they are nonnegative and sum to one.

3.7 Multinomial analysis of private car ownership

We illustrate the standard multinomial logit model by an analysis of private car ownership, based on the same data set that was used in Sections 2.7 and 2.8. The difference is that we now have four instead of two states since we distinguish three forms of private car ownership. The full count of states and their incidence among the 2820 sample households is as follows

- NONE, household does not own private car (1010, or 36%);
- USED, household owns one used private car (944, or 33%);
- NEW, household owns one new private car (691, or 25%);
- MORE, household owns more than one private car (175, or 6%).

We use the same set of explanatory variables as in Section 2.8:

- LINCEQ, the log of income per equivalent adult;
- LSIZE, the log of household size, measured by the number of equivalent adults;
- BUSCAR, a (0,1) dummy variable for the presence of a business car in the household;
- URBA, the degree of urbanisation, measured on a six-point scale from the countryside (1) to the city (6).
- HHAGE, the age of the head of the household, measured by five-year classes starting with the class 'below 20 years'.

Table 3.1 Effect of adding regressor variables on loglikelihood of multinomial car ownership model.

Number	Regressons	log L
0	Constant only	−3528.37
1	Constant, LINCEQ	−3466.80
2	Constant, LINCEQ, LSIZE	−3176.80
3	Constant, LINCEQ, LSIZE, BUSCAR	−2949.76
4	Constant, LINCEQ, LSIZE, BUSCAR, URBA	−2941.60
5	Constant, LINCEQ, LSIZE, BUSCAR, URBA, HHAGE	−2847.90

The analysis follows the same lines as in Section 2.8. In Table 3.1 we show the course of the loglikelihood function as additional regressors are successively introduced, starting from zero, i.e., the base-line model with no regressors apart from the constant. This shows the same unsteady increase as in Table 2.5 of Section 2.8, with large leaps forward upon the introduction of LSIZE and BUSCAR and a quite small contribution of URBA. Note that if we wish to test for the significance of each additional regressor by the likelihood ratio test of (2.61), as we did in discussing Table 2.5 in Section 2.8, the number of coefficients associated with each regressor is three, since we now distinguish four states. The 5% significant value of chi square with three degrees of freedom is 7.815, so that the loglikelihood should increase by at least 3.9 for each additional regressor, as it amply does.

There is a considerable difference with the bivariate case in the explanatory power of LINCEQ alone, which was quite small there (see the discussion in Section 2.7) and is now substantial. As we shall see presently, the explanation is that the income variable is a powerful determinant of ownership of new cars and of more cars, but of very little importance for the ownership of used cars, which are a major component of car ownership *per se*.

A comparison of Table 3.1 with Tables 2.4 and 2.5 for the bivariate case also shows that while the *course* of the loglikelihood function is similar, its level is quite different. This is due to the difference in the number of distinct states, as may be demonstrated for the base-line case. Its loglikelihood was given in (70) as

$$\log L^{\circ} = \sum_{s} n_s \log n_s - n \log n \tag{72}$$

Consider a given set of S states and let one state r be further subdivided into J states r_j, then (72) is increased by the negative quantity

$$\sum_{j} n_{rj} \log n_{rj} - n_r \log n_r \tag{73}$$

as inspection will confirm. This is exactly what happens in the passage from the bivariate analysis of Section 2.8 to the present multinomial analysis: the category 'private car ownership' has been further subdivided into three subclasses. Upon

Table 3.2 Income effects in the multinomial car ownership model for several sets of regressors*.

Model nr.†	NONE	USED	NEW	MORE
1	−0.08	−0.13	0.18	0.03
	(4.11)	(6.36)	(10.00)	(2.61)
2	−0.43	−0.01	0.28	0.16
	(14.60)	(0.47)	(11.44)	(11.35)
3	−0.59	0.06	0.34	0.19
	(17.04)	(1.99)	(13.10)	(12.49)
4	−0.60	0.06	0.34	0.19
	(17.07)	(2.09)	(13.12)	(12.47)
5	−0.56	0.04	0.34	0.18
	(16.29)	(1.37)	(12.90)	(12.01)

* Derivatives with respect to LINCEQ, i.e. quasi-elasticities with respect to income.
† See Table 3.1.

substituting the sample numbers given above in (73) it is found that this in itself adds -3528.38 to the base-line loglikelihood. The other loglikelihoods are changed by similar amounts, and for the same reason.

Table 3.2, which is the counterpart of Table 2.5, shows the effect of the additional regressors on the estimated income effects. Note the small effect of the income variable on the proportion of used-car owners. As more and more regressor variables are added, the *t*-ratios improve (as was to be expected), but the systematic movement away from zero from the bivariate model is not repeated. In fact the omitted variables bias of the bivariate model of Section 2.8 does not carry over to the multinomial model. To see this, we repeat the analysis of (2.100) where the omitted variables are introduced into the argument of the logit function as a separate regressor W_i. In the multinomial case, this variable must have a coefficient, say λ_s, which is normalised in the usual way with respect to the reference state, i.e. $\lambda_0 = 0$.* We thus have

$$Pl_s(\mathbf{x}_i^{\mathrm{T}}\boldsymbol{\beta}_s + \lambda_s W_i) = \exp(\mathbf{x}_i^{\mathrm{T}}\boldsymbol{\beta}_s + \lambda_s W_i) \Big/ \left(1 + \sum_{t=2}^{S} \exp(\mathbf{x}_i^{\mathrm{T}}\boldsymbol{\beta}_t + \lambda_t W_i)\right) \tag{74}$$

As before, we may expand Pl_s into a Taylor series, treat W_i as a random variable and impose $EW_i = 0$. The analogue of (2.102) is then

$$P(\mathbf{y}_i = \mathbf{i}_s) \approx Pl_s(\mathbf{x}_i^{\mathrm{T}}\boldsymbol{\beta}_s) + \tfrac{1}{2}\sigma^2 Pl(\mathbf{x}_i^{\mathrm{T}}\boldsymbol{\beta}_s)'' \tag{75}$$

In the bivariate case, the bias turned on the behaviour of the second derivative. In the present case we find

$$Pl_s(*)'' = Pl_s(*)\,.\left\{\left(\lambda_s - \sum_t \lambda_t Pl_t(*)\right)^2 - \sum_t Pl_t(*)\left(\lambda_t - \sum_t \lambda_t Pl_t(*)\right)^2\right\} \tag{76}$$

with * denoting $\mathbf{x}_i^{\mathrm{T}}\boldsymbol{\beta}_s$. We may simplify this by defining

$$\tilde{\lambda} = \sum_t \lambda_t Pl_t(*) \tag{77a}$$

$$\widetilde{\operatorname{var}}\,\lambda = \sum_t Pl_t(*)(\lambda_t - \tilde{\lambda})^2 \tag{77b}$$

for a weighted mean and variance respectively. Upon introducing these expressions, (76) read as

$$Pl_s(*)'' = Pl_s(*)\{(\lambda_s - \tilde{\lambda})^2 - \widetilde{\operatorname{var}}\,\lambda\} \tag{78}$$

Note that the weights in (77) depend on * and hence on the observation *i*. This limits the validity of the conclusion from (78) that the sign of $Pl_s(*)''$ depends on the value of λ_s relatively to the other λ_t, for both $\tilde{\lambda}$ and $\widetilde{\operatorname{var}}\,\lambda$ change from one

* Incidentally, since the scale of W_i is indeterminate, we may moreover set one nonzero λ_s equal to one.

observation to another. It would go too far to analyse this relationship; for present purposes the main point of the analysis is that the expression suggests no clear sign of $Pl_s(*)''$ for various s, and hence no simple omitted variable bias in the 'true' probability P_s of (75) and thereby in the estimated coefficients. The bias of the bivariate case thus has no equally simple counterpart in the multinomial model.

Table 3.3 Estimated coefficients of full multinomial car ownership model.*

State	LINCEQ	LSIZE	BUSCAR	URBA	HHAGE
Reference state NONE					
USED	1.69	2.55	−3.00	−0.13	−0.20
	(10.33)	(15.74)	(16.10)	(4.14)	(10.78)
NEW	2.95	2.69	−3.02	−0.11	−0.06
	(16.79)	(15.74)	(14.40)	(3.43)	(3.21)
MORE	4.52	5.84	−3.60	−0.08	−0.04
	(15.53)	(17.82)	(9.74)	(1.45)	(1.21)
Reference state USED					
NEW	1.26	0.13	−0.02	0.02	0.14
	(7.93)	(0.82)	(0.09)	(0.51)	(7.38)
MORE	2.83	3.29	−0.60	0.05	0.15
	(10.37)	(10.60)	(1.57)	(0.95)	(4.14)
Reference state NEW					
MORE	1.57	3.16	−0.57	0.03	0.01
	(5.86)	(10.19)	(1.50)	(0.64)	(0.38)

* β_s, with absolute value of t-ratio in brackets.

From these largely statistical considerations we now turn to an economic interpretation of the estimation results for the full model with all five regressors, i.e. number 5 of Table 3.1. One way of presenting the results is to give the β_s, as we do in Table 3.3. In the first part of the table the reference state is NONE, and in the later parts we change to other reference states; this arrangement permits the comparison of any pair of states. While the coefficients in each further set are easily obtained by taking differences from the preceding set, as can be seen from (8), the t-values are not so readily constructed, and can only be obtained by applying (2.59) to the full covariance matrix of the original estimates.

According to the discrete choice argument, each row of coefficients shows the effect of the regressors on the utility of the state under consideration, relatively to the utility of the reference state. Coefficients close to zero indicate that the regressor concerned does not affect the utility (nor the probability) of the state to which it applies, relatively to the reference state. In the top part of Table 3.3, income, household size and the presence of a business car all affect the utility of any type of car ownership vis-à-vis non-ownership; but urbanisation and age, while of some importance for single-car ownership (whether used or new), do not discriminate between non-owners and multiple car owners. When we continue downward in the table, the other two sets show the effect of regressors between specific car ownership categories. Income is always a potent factor, but household size is only important for the number of cars, not for the choice between new and used cars. The presence of a business car and the degree of urbanisation do affect private car ownership *per se*, but not its form. Age finally does discriminate between ownership of a single used car and the two other ownership classes, but not between the latter two. The last row once more confirms the importance of income and household size, and the lack of importance of the other three variables.

On the whole, then, a plausible pattern emerges from considerations of significance of the β coefficients for various alternative reference states. To show the simultaneous effect of the regressor variables on the probabilities of the four distinct states we should however turn to the derivatives of (16). These need not have the same sign as the corresponding β_s, as inspection of that expression shows, and as a comparison of Tables 3.3 and 3.4 confirms. The variances of these derivatives, and hence their *t*-values, have again been calculated according to (2.59). The result is shown in Table 3.4.

Table 3.4 Effects of regressor variables on private car ownership status.*

	NONE	USED	NEW	MORE
LINCEQ	−0.56	0.04	0.34	0.18
	(16.29)	(1.37)	(12.90)	(12.01)
LSIZE	−0.67	0.23	0.20	0.25
	(19.83)	(7.56)	(7.60)	(13.98)
BUSCAR	0.70	−0.35	−0.26	−0.10
	(19.66)	(8.67)	(6.99)	(4.86)
URBA	0.03	−0.02	−0.01	−0.00
	(4.21)	(3.11)	(1.82)	(0.08)
HHAGE	0.03	−0.04	0.01	0.00
	(8.22)	(10.74)	(2.05)	(1.16)

* Derivatives at the sample mean.

Since both the income and the household size variable are taken in logarithms, the derivatives correspond to quasi-elasticities. The effect of income per head is generally lower than that of size, and the ownership of used cars is not affected by income changes at all. A business car again turns out to be a perfect substitute for any private car, with derivatives of probabilities in respect of this dummy approximately equal to the sample frequency or mean probability of the ownership category concerned. Urbanisation and age have minor; but significant effects on non-ownership versus the ownership of a used car.

We must emphasise that all effects have been measured at the mean sample frequencies of the four ownership states, and that this gives a narrow view of the variation that the regressors may engender. When the regressor variables range over a wider region, the outcome can be quite different. In the present case the low income elasticity of used-car ownership arises largely because at the sample mean frequencies the probability of used-car ownership happens to be almost at its peak. Figure 3.2 shows how the four probabilities are affected when income varies over a wide range, with all other regressor variables kept constant at their sample mean values. The sample mean for *all* regressors obtains when income (per equivalent adult) is about Fl. 7500, and this is close but not identical to the sample frequencies (because of the nonlinearity of the model); at this value, USED is almost at its maximum. The income values at the lower end of the graph are admittedly unrealistic, but we see clearly how the USED category first increases at the expense of NONE and then declines because it is overtaken by NEW. This also illustrates that the multinomial probabilities do not vary monotonically with the regressor variables, in contrast to the bivariate model. But the interest of Fig. 3.2 does not lie only in the behaviour of USED but in the overall picture of how the probabilities change as income increases.

Another way of demonstrating the implications of the estimated model is to work out the estimated probabilities for several stereotype households. In Table 3.5, the first two columns serve to illustrate the discrepancy between the mean sample frequencies and the probabilities at the sample mean values of the regressors. In the other two columns, we present the result for two households. Household A is a large family with a young father, a modest income, living in the country; B is a much older pair, quite well-to-do and living in a large city. Neither household has a business car. The contrast in car ownership probabilities is striking. The poor countryside family is actually more likely to own a car than the rich city dwellers, but it goes for used cars while the latter have a strong preference for a new car. The differences between the two families may actually be split up and attributed to the various aspects in which they differ.

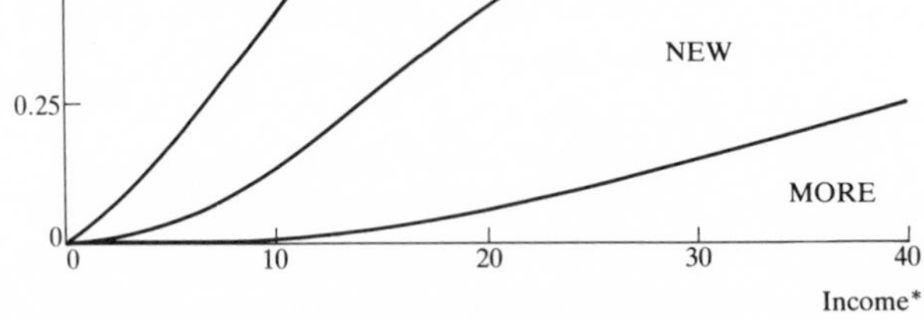

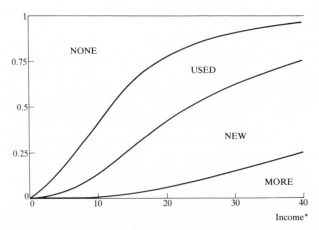

Fig. 3.2 Car ownership probabilities as a function of income.
*Income per equivalent adult × Fl.10 p.a.

Table 3.5 Private car ownership status probabilities at selected regressor values.

	Mean frequencies	Sample mean	*A*	*B*
Regressor values*:				
1. Income		15.74†	6.0	25.0
2. Size		2.12†	4.0	1.7
3. Business car		0.12	0	0
4. Urbanisation		3.74	1	6
5. Age of head		45	22.5	52.5
	Frequencies or probabilities (%)			
Private car ownership status:				
NONE	35.8	33.6	14.3	24.5
USED	33.5	36.7	74.7	26.0
NEW	24.5	27.1	9.4	43.4
MORE	6.2	3.1	1.6	6.1

* 1. In Fl. 1,000 p.a. per equivalent adult.
2. Number of equivalent adults.
3. (0,1) dummy.
4. Six classes from 1 country to 6 city.
5. Years, based on mid-points of five-year classes.

† Geometric means.

We shall not take this analysis further; with a full regiment of households from all walks of life, we would come close to simulating the car ownership for a group or (sub)population, and this is the subject of Chapter 5.

4

Further Developments of the Model

4.1 The conditional logit model

In the standard logit model of the last chapter, the general formula (3.10)

$$P_{is} = \exp(V_{is}) / \sum_t \exp(V_{it}) \tag{1}$$

is completed by the restrictive specification (3.15)

$$V_{is} = \mathbf{x}_i^{\mathrm{T}} \boldsymbol{\gamma}_s \tag{2}$$

The regressor variables $\mathbf{x}_i$ are **generic** characteristics of i, the conditions of an experiment, or the covariates of a particular observation, with the same value for all states or options s; the coefficients $\boldsymbol{\gamma}_s$ are **state dependent** or **(state) specific**, so that the regressors do not affect all states in the same way. The $\boldsymbol{\gamma}_s$ of (2) were then **normalized** in the interest of identification, and this led to (3.9):

$$V_{is} = \mathbf{x}_i^{\mathrm{T}} \boldsymbol{\beta}_s \text{ for } s = 1, \tag{3a}$$

$$\boldsymbol{\beta}_1 = \mathbf{0}, \qquad \text{or } V_{i1} = 1 \text{ for all } i. \tag{3b}$$

We now specify V_{is} instead as a function of a vector of **state-dependent** or **specific** variables $\mathbf{z}_{is}$. These regressors represent aspects or properties of the various states s that vary with the conditions of observation i, or aspects or properties of observation i that vary according to the state s, which comes to the same thing. If s denotes a mode of travel, and i a particular trip, $\mathbf{z}_{is}$ lists characteristics like speed, cost, waiting time, and travel time of each mode s for trip i; and these vary with the trips' coordinates, like the itinerary, the time of the day, the number of travellers, and so on. In the case of college choice by freshmen, $\mathbf{z}_{is}$ lists distance, cost, and admission facilities for each college s from the viewpoint of individual i. Such variables differ between modes and between observations, hence the double suffixes i and s of $\mathbf{z}$; in fact we reserve this notation for variables that do exhibit both types of variation in the observed sample. There is a distinct vector $\mathbf{z}$ for every combination of i and s, and for every observation i there are as many vectors $\mathbf{z}_{is}$ as there are modes s.

The first specification depends *exclusively* on specific regressors, with common coefficients $\boldsymbol{\alpha}$, or

$$V_{is} = \mathbf{z}_{is}^{\mathrm{T}} \boldsymbol{\alpha} \tag{4}$$

This is the (pure) **conditional logit** model of McFadden (1974), who introduced it in conjuction with the discrete choice theory of Section 3.3. In that theory V_{is} is the systematic component of utility of mode s in situation i, and this utility interpretation of discrete choice is indeed well suited to this model, much more so than to the standard multinomial logit. An interesting and convincing example of both ideas is the early study of travel behaviour of Washington commuters by Lerman and Ben-Akiva (1976). They distinguish five modes s which are a combination of household car ownership and car used, such as 'two cars, but not used for travel to work'. The utility of each mode depends on variables like travel time, a combined variable for income and specific mode travel costs, and the ratio of cars to licensed drivers in the household, with a different definition for car-to-work modes and others. These and other variables testify to the ingenuity of the analysts.

The assumption in (4) of a *common* $\boldsymbol{\alpha}$ for all states is only natural if it is believed that aspects like costs, travel time, and distance, if properly measured, affect the utility of all transport modes for a given trip in the same way. Note that there is no need to normalise $\boldsymbol{\alpha}$ for identification. The terms of $\mathbf{z}_{is}^{\mathrm{T}}\boldsymbol{\alpha}$ correspond to the contribution of each aspect to the overall utility V_{is} of a given mode, and the elements of $\boldsymbol{\alpha}$ indicate the relative weight of these aspects. We may for instance compare the coefficients of cost and speed, which affect utility with opposite sign: their ratio marks the trade-off of cost and speed at constant utility, and shows how much a traveller is willing to pay for a given saving in time.

Apart from this easy interpretation of elements of $\boldsymbol{\alpha}$, the conditional logit model (4) also permits extrapolation to a new mode v with known characteristics $\mathbf{z}_{iv}$ for each i. Once $\boldsymbol{\alpha}$ has been estimated, we can calculate V_{iv} as $\mathbf{z}_{iv}^{\mathrm{T}}\boldsymbol{\alpha}$ and insert this in (1). This is useful when the introduction of a new mode of transport or of some other option is contemplated, and its uncertain performance is under debate. Note however that this is precisely the type of application where the defects of the independence from irrelevant alternatives (IIA) property are most keenly felt, as the usual demonstration of the property by the blue bus–red bus argument shows. As we have seen in Section 3.2, the IIA holds for any multinomial logit model, regardless of the specification of the V_{is}, and it also applies here.

The underlying idea of the *pure* conditional logit model (4) is that the (systematic component of) utility V_{is} can be completely described by the $\mathbf{z}_{is}$. This resembles the view of all commodities as bundles of properties that make up their utility, earlier advocated by Lancaster (1971) as a general approach to the theory of consumer demand. It is not entirely compatible with the introduction of specific regressors $\mathbf{z}_{is}$ along with the generic regressors $\mathbf{x}_i$, to begin with the dummy constant '1'. By its definition, $\mathbf{z}_{is}$ contains no such variable, and $\boldsymbol{\alpha}$ no intercept. If we wish to add these, (4) is replaced by

$$V_{is} = \beta_s^{\circ} + \mathbf{z}_{is}^{\mathrm{T}}\boldsymbol{\alpha} \tag{5a}$$

$$\beta_1^{\circ} = 0 \tag{5b}$$

The intercepts β_s°, like all specific coefficients attached to generic variables, do need normalisation, so that we have only $(S-1)$ different parameters. At times it may be convenient to include these in an extended vector of common coefficients, say α^*; this is accomplished by defining specific (0,1) dummies for each of the $(S-1)$ states. For an example, see Table 4.2 in Section 4.3 below.

In (5), the intercepts β_s° reflect the intrinsic or unique utility of each mode s, relative to mode 1, after taking into account their known qualities listed in the $\mathbf{z}_{is}$. It is no longer pretended that these observed qualities completely determine utility. This is probably more realistic than the pure model (4), but it raises an awkward problem in the extrapolation to a new mode v, since we have no basis for the value of β_v° that must be assumed.

We may also of course combine any numbers of generic and specific regressor variables, as in

$$V_{is} = \mathbf{x}_i^{\mathrm{T}}\boldsymbol{\beta}_s + \mathbf{z}_{is}^{\mathrm{T}}\boldsymbol{\alpha} \tag{6a}$$

$$\boldsymbol{\beta}_1 = \mathbf{0} \tag{6b}$$

with all coefficients of the generic regressors normalised. The utility model still holds, but perceived utility is now controlled for the conditions of each observation, as described by the covariates $\mathbf{x}_i$. The extrapolation to a new mode v will accordingly require assumptions about all elements of $\boldsymbol{\beta}_v$.

The properties of the conditional logit model—with or without the addition of generic regressors—are easily derived. For the derivative of the probabilities in respect of an element Z of $\mathbf{z}$ with coefficient α we find at a given observation or at given conditions i

$$\partial P_{is}/\partial Z_{is} = \alpha P_{is}(1 - P_{is}) \tag{7a}$$

$$\partial P_{is}/\partial Z_{it} = -\alpha P_{is} P_{it} \tag{7b}$$

These derivatives can of course also be evaluated at the sample mean, with the mean probabilities or sample frequencies substituted into (7). In the derivatives shown, P_{is} is for instance the probability of car travel and P_{it} the probability of public transport for a particular trip i, and the Z's are their respective speeds. We see that the probabilities vary monotonically with each specific regressor.* The sign depends on α; for positive qualities, like speed, α is positive, and for Zs like cost and loss of time α is negative. By (7), the effects on P_{is} of changes in its own Z_{is} and in other states' Z_{it} alternate in sign. Thus P_{is} declines upon an increase in its own cost, and increases upon cost rises of other modes.

We note the symmetry of (7b), whereby

$$\partial P_{is}/\partial Z_{it} = \partial P_{it}/\partial Z_{is} \tag{8}$$

It is easly verified that

$$\sum_s \partial P_{is}/\partial Z_{it} = 0 \tag{9}$$

* In the standard model, probabilities vary monotonically with generic regressors in the bivariate case, but not in the multinomial model. See Sections 2.1 and 3.2, Figs. 2.2 and 3.2.

as well as

$$\sum_t \partial P_{is}/\partial Z_{it} = 0 \tag{10}$$

The first expression states the obvious (that the probabilities always sum to one), the second shows that the probabilities remain the same upon the same change in Z_t or Z_{it} for all t, as they should. For if all Z_{it} change by the same amount, all utilities V_{is} also change by the same factor, and this does not affect the preferred choice at observation i.

Quasi-elasticities are obtained as before by multiplying the derivatives (7) by the relevant values of Z_{is} or Z_{it}, or

$$\eta_{ss} = \alpha Z_{is} P_{is}(1 - P_{is}) \tag{11a}$$

$$\eta_{st} = -\alpha Z_{it} P_{it} P_{is} \tag{11b}$$

4.2 Estimation

We return once more to the *scoring* variant of maximum likelihood estimation, defined by the iterative scheme of (2.60) or (3.49),

$$\boldsymbol{\theta}_{t+1} = \boldsymbol{\theta}_t + \mathbf{H}(\boldsymbol{\theta}_t)^{-1}\mathbf{q}(\boldsymbol{\theta}_t) \tag{12}$$

For multinomial probability models in general, the score vector $\mathbf{q}$ and the information matrix $\mathbf{H}$ have been derived in general terms in Section 3.5, with the derivatives of the probabilities in respect of the parameters still to be inserted. The vector and the matrix are obtained by summation over i of $\mathbf{q}_i$ and $\mathbf{H}_i$, and we shall first consider these expressions, which refer to the ith observation. For any two parameters θ_h, θ_m of some multinomial probability model a typical element of $\mathbf{q}_i$ was given in (3.52) as

$$q_{ih} = \sum_s \frac{Y_{is}}{P_{is}} \frac{\partial P_{is}}{\partial \theta_h} \tag{13}$$

and a typical element of H_i in (3.55) as

$$H_{ihm} = \sum_s \frac{1}{P_{is}} \cdot \frac{\partial P_{is}}{\partial \theta_h} \cdot \frac{\partial P_{is}}{\partial \theta_m} \tag{14}$$

All we need to complete these expressions is the derivatives of the probabilities in respect of the parameters. For the pure conditional logit model (4) this is

$$\partial P_{is}/\partial \alpha_h = P_{is}(Z_{ish} - \sum_t Z_{ith} P_{it}) \tag{15}$$

We may define a weighted average of the Z_{ish} for observation i, say

$$\bar{Z}_{ih} = \sum_t P_{it} Z_{ith} \tag{16}$$

and rewrite (15) as

$$\partial P_{is}/\partial \alpha_h = P_{is}(Z_{ish} - \bar{Z}_{ih}) \tag{17}$$

From (13) we then find for a typical element of $\mathbf{q}_{i\alpha}$

$$q_{i\alpha h} = \sum_s Y_{is}(Z_{ish} - \bar{Z}_{ih}) \tag{18}$$

Note that the summation over s yields only a single nonzero term, as all but one of the Y_{is} are zero. For an element of $H_{i\alpha}$ we obtain, from (14),

$$H_{i\alpha hm} = \sum_s P_{is}(Z_{ish} - \bar{Z}_{ih})(Z_{ism} - \bar{Z}_{ih}) \tag{19}$$

which looks like a weighted moment. The weights P_{is} vary of course with the parameters that are being estimated; but in an iterative scheme this is quite common.

If we wish to estimate the full model (6), $\mathbf{q}_i$ and H_i can be partitioned as

$$\mathbf{q}_i = \begin{bmatrix} \mathbf{q}_{i\beta} \\ \mathbf{q}_{i\alpha} \end{bmatrix} \tag{20}$$

and

$$\mathbf{H}_i = \begin{bmatrix} \mathbf{H}_{i\beta\beta} & \mathbf{H}_{i\beta\alpha} \\ \mathbf{H}_{i\beta\alpha} & \mathbf{H}_{i\alpha\alpha} \end{bmatrix} \tag{21}$$

The terms in β have been given in Section 3.6, equations (3.61) and (3.65); the terms in α have just been derived; for the off-diagonal matrices of $\mathbf{H}$, the derivatives of (3.59) and of (17) must be substituted into (14). This presents no particular difficulties.

If the choice set varies between observations, summation over s for each i should take place over a set S_i that varies from one observation to another. Differences in the choice set will also affect $\mathbf{q}_{i\beta}$ and the elements of $\mathbf{H}_i$ that involve the β parameters, as the absence of a state implies the absence of a subset of $\boldsymbol{\beta}$, and zero elements in the corresponding places. But this is a matter of careful programming which raises no questions of principle.

Finally, summation over i will yield the expressions that must be inserted into (12) to complete the estimation algorithm.

4.3 Choice of a mode of payment*

We illustrate the conditional model by an application to the choice of a mode of payment by customers for payments made in shops, restaurants and bars. Such **point of sale payments** by anonymous clients demand immediate and secure settlement. Bank transfers are therefore out of the question, and in practice currency or guaranteed cheques are the only form of payment acceptable to the

*The following example has been taken from a study originally commissioned by the Dutch Postbank, and earlier reported in Mot *et al.* (1989).

creditor. The analysis refers to the Netherlands in 1987, and at that time the role of credit cards was negligible. There were however three types of guaranteed cheques current, with slightly different properties. The purpose of the study is to ascertain the determinants of the choice between cash and these three types of cheque. Such information is of great interest to the banks in setting the conditions of use for the cheques they issue, and for the design of new modes of payment such as electronic cards.

The data were taken from the Dutch Intomart household expenditure panel. In addition to the usual information of a family budget survey, this panel records the mode of payment (cash, cheque, direct debiting and so on) of each item of expenditure as well as other details like the person making the purchase and the place of payment (shop, bank, home). We use a data set which is a random sample of about 3000 from all payments in 1987 by the 1000 households participating in the panel.* The present analysis is restricted to a subsample of 2161 payments made in shops, restaurants and bars, and paid for in cash or by handing over a guaranteed cheque. We use currency and cash indiscriminately to designate banknotes and coins. There are three types of cheques, each guaranteeing payment to the recipient up to a certain limit, provided the cheque is accompanied by a bank card when it is signed. We shall distinguish these three types by their colour. The *green* cheque, issued by the commerical banks, is guaranteed for sums up to Fl. 100, roughly the equivalent of $50. The *orange* cheque of the postal giro system has an upper limit of Fl. 200. The *blue* Eurocheque is issued by the banks, like the green cheque, and it has an upper limit of Fl. 300. Access to the blue cheque, which is also valid in other European countries, is somewhat limited, and there is a small charge for it. All limits apply to a single cheque, and larger sums may be paid by writing several cheques. Very nearly all Dutch households (and all households in our sample) have an account with the postal giro system and/or with one or more banks, with the giro most widely prevalent among all classes of society. All three types of cheque are thus in principle available to all households, and in fact very many of them have more than one account, and many of them have more than one type of cheque. In analysing the mode of payment, we shall assume that the four modes of payment (cash and cheques of three colours) are available to all payees, although this is not strictly true; we should have allowed for variations in the choice set in regard of the cheques a household has at its disposal, but the data set does not permit this.

The vast majority of payments at the point of sale is made in currency or cash, as can be seen from the compositon of the sample:

total number of payments	2161
of which in currency	1845
green cheque	25
yellow cheque	99
blue cheque	67

* The survey records only one in ten of small expenditures below Fl. 10, but we have redressed this in drawing the subsample.

It is a pity that cash payments dominate the sample to such an extent; for an analysis of the mode of payment we would prefer a much larger spread of payments over the various modes. As Table 4.1 shows, the prevalence of cash reflects that most payments are for small amounts, and that small amounts are usually paid in cash.

Table 4.1 Point of sale payments by mode and size (Dutch survey of 1987).

		Guaranteed cheque		
	Cash	green	orange	blue
Number of observations	1845	25	99	67
			column percentage	
⩽Fl. 100	97.2	78.1	73.6	67.7
Fl. 100—⩽Fl. 200	2.2	18.8	17.6	25.3
Fl. 200—⩽ Fl. 300	0.4	3.2	4.6	3.0
Over Fl. 300	0.3	—	2.3	4.0

Several varieties of the logit model can be used to analyse this relation between the size and the mode of payment. The simplest approach is a standard multinomial model which serves for description. This is *model A* with four states for the four modes of payment and a single regressor apart from the constant, namely the amount paid, in logarithms. The use of the logarithm is a purely empirical matter: it substantially improves the fit as measured by the loglikelihood.

The result of estimating this model A are given in the top part of Table 4.3. We find a strong relationship whereby small amounts are paid in cash and larger amounts by cheque, and we also obtain quasi-elasticities for each mode in respect of the size of the payment. As the amount increases, the use of currency is reduced that of each cheque increased, but not in the same degree. The low elasticity of green cheques reflects their limited range.

This is what one would expect from Table 4.1. It also confirms casual observation and introspection. But *why* should people prefer to pay small amounts in cash and use cheques only for larger sums? We shall attribute this choice to the generalised transaction cost of the four modes of payment under consideration, represented by their **risk** and **inconvenience**. These are two independent aspects of each mode of payment, and we shall enter them as separate determinants of the mode's utility in a conditional logit model.

By **risk** we mean the dangers of theft and loss attached to a mode. For currency, it is a function of the sum paid, for this determines the amount of cash one has to carry; more precisely, we assume that the risk of using currency is proportional to the log of payment size. For guaranteed cheques, risk is the perceived cost of losing cheques and/or the accompanying bank card. This is limited to a fixed amount, depending on the exact circumstances of losing cheques or card, but these precise rules are not widely known to the public. We assume that the perceived risk is constant and the same for all three cheque types. As for **inconvenience**, we measure this as the number of signatures required. For currency, it is zero, regardless of the size of the payment; for cheques, it is equal to the number of cheques required to pay a given sum, which is

amount to be paid **modulo** upper cheque limit.

Note that inconvenience varies with the size of the payment but also with the colour of the cheque.*

Table 4.2 Definition of variables in conditional logit model.

	Cash	Guaranteed cheque		
		green	orange	blue
Model B				
*Risk of cash	logsize	0	0	0
of cheque	0	1	1	1
Inconvenience	0	size *mod* 100	size *mod* 200	size *mod* 300
Model C				
Intercept 1	0	1	0	0
2	0	0	1	0
3	0	0	0	1
Risk of cash	logsize	0	0	0
Inconvenience	0	size *mod* 100	size *mod* 200	size *mod* 300

*The estimated coefficient of the cheque risk dummies represents the constant cheque risk.

Table 4.2 sets out the definition of these two specific variables. They are first used in a pure conditional logit model of the form (4), labelled *model B*. It contains no intercept, and allows for no differences between the three cheques apart from their guaranteed face value, and hence their inconvenience.

Since this is unrealistic, we have added a third model (*model C*) which is a conditional logit model with a generic dummy constant 1, and specific intercepts, as in (5). Normalisation sets the intercept at zero for the reference mode, which is cash. In order to bring out the structure of the model, we have rewritten the regressor variables corresponding to the specific intercepts as if they were specific regressor variables, each with its own (generic) coefficient. This is shown in Table 4.2. It will be appreciated that the constant cheque risk is no longer identified. We shall therefore equate it to the mean intercept of the three cheques, and then interpret the deviations from this mean as the relative intrinsic utility of each cheque mode.

* Since bank clients receive a limited number of cheques at a time, the tendency to reserve the use of cheques for larger amounts may also be explained by a stock management model whereby the payee at each payment maximises the remaining time his stocks of cheques and currency will last. We have not pursued this idea.

Table 4.3 Estimates of three modes of payment models.

A. Standard logit in logsize		
6 parameters	$\log L = -826.55$	
Quasi-elasticities with respect to size:		
	currency	−0.18 (16.8)
cheques	green	0.02 (6.6)
	orange	0.08 (13.1)
	blue	0.07 (12.3)
B. Conditional logit, without intercepts		
3 parameters	$\log L = -839.12$	
Coefficients of	currency risk	−1.86 (18.0)
	cheque risk	−8.44 (20.4)
	inconvenience	−1.17 (5.0)
C. Conditional logit, with intercepts		
5 parameters	$\log L = -816.55$	
Coefficients of	currency risk	−1.79 (17.4)
	inconvenience	−0.91 (4.0)
Intercepts of cheques	green	−9.25 (21.0)
	orange	−8.04 (19.5)
	blue	−8.39 (20.2)

Absolute t-values in brackets.
Base-line loglikelihood −1052.68.

The results of fitting the three models are shown in Table 4.3. We have already briefly commented above on the estimates of model A. The first conditional model, B, also has quite precise coefficient estimates (always judged by their t-values). It has a worse fit than A, according to its loglikelihood; but then it has less parameters. Likelihood ratio tests cannot be used in this context, for model B is not nested within A (nor is the base-line model nested within B, which has no intercepts). The coefficient of cash risk is a quasi-elasticity (since we use logsize), and the risk attached to the use of cheques is

$$\exp(-8.44/-1.86) = \text{Fl. } 93.50$$

which is a quite acceptable result.

As for model C, it yields equally precise estimates as A and B, and the fit is better than that of A, in spite of a smaller number of parameters. The coefficients of cash risk and of inconvenience are not substantially different from B. If we identify cheque risk with the weighted mean of the intercepts, its coefficient is −8.32, or the equivalent of

$$\exp(-8.32/-1.79) = \text{Fl. } 104.50$$

near enough to the earlier estimate. The specific utility of the three cheques is then represented by the deviation of their intercept from this weighted mean, or

green cheque	−0.93
orange cheque	0.28
blue cheque	−0.07

This brings out that if we allow for inconvenience and assume there is no difference in risk, orange cheques are by far the most popular of the three, with blue cheques following closely and green cheques at a considerable distance. These effects may be translated into differences in choice probabilities, or in frequencies of use, for particular payments i, that is for payments of a given size.

The major advantage of the conditional logit model is in its use for assessing the likely effect of policy changes, such as a reduction in the own risk of cheques, or changes in the guaranteed limits. In order to assess these effects, we may introduce these changes in the model by redefining the variables of Table 4.2 accordingly, recalculating the probabilities of the four payment modes for all payments in the sample, and summing over the sample. We return to these methods of conditional prediction in Section 5.2.

4.4 General linear form of the argument

With a little ingenuity in defining variables and selecting parameters, there is a great deal of freedom in the specification of the logit argument V_{is}; expression (6), which combines generic and specific regressors, is by no means the most general specification. We shall explore the possibilities that are open to the analyst. The discussion is restricted to linear functions of the regressor variables with constant coefficients—nonlinear expressions of the same variables seldom offer a substantial improvement. The only logical limitation is that the parameters of the linear combination V_{is} must be identified for given probabilities (1), that is

$$P_{is} = \exp(V_{is}) / \sum_t \exp(V_{it}) \tag{22}$$

The principal distinction among regressor variables is by their *variation* across observations i and/or states s. We list four classes, each reserved for variables that do in fact exhibit the sample variation that is indicated by their suffixes. The first class consists of the *specific* regressor vectors $\mathbf{z}_{is}$ which vary with i and, for each i, with s. An example is travel time which varies both with the distance of the trip i and with the mode of transport s. Secondly, there are *generic* regressor vectors $\mathbf{x}_i$ that vary with i but not with s, such as the trip distance or the age or income class of the traveller. These are constants for each observation. Note that $\mathbf{x}_i$ is here expressly restricted to variables that do indeed vary between observations; in contrast to earlier usage it does not include a dummy constant '1'. The third class consists of **state constants** $\mathbf{w}_s$ that vary only between states or modes but not between observations, like the comfort or safety of a mode of transport, or its fixed costs. These three classes refer to regressor variables that have actually been observed. The fourth category consists of a single scalar c, the **dummy constant**, which takes the same value (usually '1') for all observations and all states. This is an artefact of the analyst, designed to allow for intercepts. The use of specific or generic dummy variables that are 1 for one observation or one state and 0 for all others is discussed presently.

The most general specification of V_{is} is a linear function of *all* available regressor variables for observation i, with *all* specific variables entering into the expression for each state. To bring out the range of the analysts' choices, we at first allow for as many separate parameters as we can think of, that is different parameters for each state s.* Taking the variables in reverse order as given above, the result is

$$V_{is} = c\beta_s^{\circ} + \mathbf{w}_s^{\mathrm{T}}\boldsymbol{\delta}_s + \mathbf{x}_i^{\mathrm{T}}\boldsymbol{\beta}_s + \sum_t \mathbf{z}_{it}^{\mathrm{T}}\boldsymbol{\alpha}_{ts} \tag{23}$$

where the scalar c is 1 and β_s° is a state-dependent intercept. The third term is familiar, but note in the fourth that all specific regressors enter into V_{is} for each state with a full set of parameters.

The form of (23) is simplified and the number of parameters reduced by the requirements of **identification**. First, there must be identification with respect to V_{is}, i.e. it must be impossible to change parameters without affecting the value of V_{is}. As a result, we can not at the same time have $c\beta_s^{\circ}$ and $\mathbf{w}_s^{\mathrm{T}}\boldsymbol{\delta}_s$, as in (23). This conflict is resolved by imposing a single $\boldsymbol{\delta}$ for all modes, as in

$$V_{is} = c\beta_s^{\circ} + \mathbf{w}_s^{\mathrm{T}}\boldsymbol{\delta} + \mathbf{x}_i^{\mathrm{T}}\boldsymbol{\beta}_s + \sum_t \mathbf{z}_{it}^{\mathrm{T}}\boldsymbol{\alpha}_{ts} \tag{24}$$

The second condition of identification refers to P_{is} of (22): by its definition we may not have identical elements for each i in all V_{is}, and changes in a parameter may not lead to equal additive changes in all V_{is}. This calls for restrictions on the S specific parameters of variables that occur in all V_{is}, as all regressors of (23) do. The $\boldsymbol{\delta}_s$ of (23) have already been restricted to a single $\boldsymbol{\delta}$ in (24); all other coefficients must be normalised by putting

$$\beta_1^{\circ} = 0, \qquad \boldsymbol{\beta}_1 = \mathbf{0}, \qquad \boldsymbol{\alpha}_{t1} = \mathbf{0} \tag{25}$$

where 1 is the arbitrary reference state.

Technically, the common dummy c or '1' with its coefficients β_s° (for $s \neq 1$) may be replaced by a set of $(S-1)$ state specific dummy vectors $\mathbf{c}_s$ which have 1 in the sth position and zeros elsewhere, with each a separate coefficient β_s° which now applies to all states. This device has already been noted in connection with equation (5), and it has been put into practice in the mode of payment analysis of Table 4.2, model C.†

I do not think that there is an identifiable linear specification that is more general than (25). With S states and k, l and m elements in the vectors $\mathbf{w}_s$, $\mathbf{x}_i$ and $\mathbf{z}_{is}$

* It will be clear that there is no point in having separate parameters for each observation. We also exclude some form of structured variation of individual parameters, so as to allow for heterogeneity.

respectively, (23) has $S \times (1 + k + l + m)$ parameters; the exigencies of identification reduce this number to $(S - 1) \times (1 + l + m) + k$ in (25). This is still a very large number, and it never arises in practice. All models reviewed earlier are special cases of this expression, and so are most specifications encountered in the literature. The further restrictions that have been imposed are a matter of the analysts' choice, and reflect assumptions of substance about the choice process under review rather than considerations of statistical expediency.

All the models considered so far have $\boldsymbol{\delta} = \mathbf{0}$, for no state constants have been encountered (although the convenience variable in the mode of payment example came near). In the models with specific regressors like (4), (5) and (6), only a single term from the last sum of (25) is retained, putting $\boldsymbol{\alpha}_{ts} = 0$ for all $t \neq s$. The remaining $\boldsymbol{\alpha}_{ss}$ are moreover restricted to a common value $\boldsymbol{\alpha}$ for all s. This is reasonable, for if the elements of the $\mathbf{z}_{is}$ correctly measure identical qualities like the speed or cost of various modes of travel for the same trip, there is no reason why, say, car costs should affect utility differently from public transport costs. Finally, in the standard model of Chapter 3, all coefficients other than the β_s° and $\boldsymbol{\beta}_s$ of (25) have been put equal to zero. This simplification is of course usually due to the absence of specific variables from the sample observations, although at times these can be created with a little imagination by the analyst.

As a rule, therefore, there are good reasons why so many current models use parsimonious specifications in comparison to the very rich parametrisation of (25) that is in principle possible. Since all these models are nested within (25), we can in principle test whether these restrictive simplifications are acceptable by the likelihood ratio test of Section 2.4, equation (2.61). Note, however, that the models are not always nested within each other; we can not for instance test the standard logit against the conditional logit in this way—although one is of course tempted to look at the size of the respective loglikelihoods, taking into account the number of parameters of each model. We return to the subject in Section 5.4.

4.5 The nested logit model

With all the generalisations so far envisaged, the original simple bivariate logit model of Chapter 2 has been extended almost beyond recognition. Even so all the above models are based, within the discrete choice framework, on a number of common restrictive assumptions that can be challenged. Recall that utility consists of a systematic component and an additive random term, as in (3.23),

$$U_{is} = V_{is} + \varepsilon_{is} \tag{26}$$

In the derivation of the logit model from maximisation of this utility in Section

† One might also think of introducing an **observation dummy** c_i that is 1 for observation i and zero elsewhere. If this is coupled with a (normalised) coefficient vector $\boldsymbol{\lambda}$, the intended results is a perfect fit for observation i. In practice, however, maximum likelihood estimation of such a model breaks down: P_i tends towards a vector with 1 for the observed state and zeros elsewhere, which maximizes $\log L_i$, but this requires the estimate of at least one element of $\boldsymbol{\lambda}$ to tend towards infinity. A much simpler (and equivalent) solution is to delete the ith observation altogether from the analysis.

3.3, a number of assumptions were made about the random disturbance. These are

1. the nature of its distribution (an extreme value distribution, with the Normal a likely alternative);
2. independence across s (with its attendant IIA property of the ensuing probability model);
3. standardisation in respect of the mean;
4. standardisation in respect of the variance (there is no room for heteroskedasticity).

There are also restrictions on the specification of the systematic part V_{is}. Apart from the obvious examples of parsimonious parametrization listed in the preceding section, there is the fundamental limitation to constant parameters that apply to all i, or the neglect of any heterogeneity in individual behaviour. Altogether, a great deal of further generalisation is possible, and some of it is under way—see Steckel and Vanhonacker (1988).

We here briefly discuss only a single generalisation, namely the **nested logit model**, which does away with the IIA property by recognising the existence of subgroups or **clusters** within the S states. Such as subset consists of alternatives or states that are similar, and in the discrete choice formulation this means that the utilities are no longer stochastically independent but correlated through correlation of the random disturbances ε_{is} across s. V_{is} is of course the same nonrandom, systematic component of utility as before. There may be several clusters, each composed of several alternatives, with correlated utilities within each cluster but independence between the utilities of (states of) different clusters.

This model is once again due to McFadden (1977; see Section 5.15 for the theory and Appendix 5.22 for estimation). The probability model is derived from utility maximisation under an assumed distribution of the random disturbances ε_s, as in Section 3.3. This is the **generalised extreme value** (GEV) distribution, which is a close generalisation of the Type I extreme value distribution (3.32). We consider the joint distribution of the ε_s of r alternatives, labelled from 1 to r_l, that together constitute the cluster l. This is given by

$$F(\varepsilon_1, \ldots, \varepsilon_{r_l}) = \exp \alpha_l \left\{ \sum_t^{r_l} \exp - \rho_l^{-1} \varepsilon_l \right\}^{\rho_l} \tag{27}$$

For the joint distribution of all disturbances we multiply these expressions over the clusters (that is: sum the exponents), since the utilities between clusters are stochastically independent. Note that the α_l and ρ_l are specific for the cluster considered. The latter parameter is associated with the dependence among the utilities of the cluster. It is constrained to lie between 0 and 1, and the correlation between any two disturbances is $1 - \rho^2$. Thus (in spite of the notation, which suggests the reverse) the limiting case of $\rho = 1$ corresponds to independent utilities as in the usual multinomial logit with the IIA property. It is sometimes suggested that the other extreme of $\rho = 0$, or perfect correlation of the disturbances, corresponds to identical alternatives; but this would also require that they have identical systematic components.

This is the **nested logit** model. In the example of car ownership we might replace the standard multinomial model for four ownership categories of Section 3.6 by this model, recognising that there is a close relation between a household's appreciation of car ownership in any form (old car, new car or more cars). The three car ownership modes then form a cluster with correlated utilities, and the other cluster consists of the single option of having no car. The multinomial logit and the nested logit are sometimes contrasted by illustrations like Figure 4.1. Note however that the nested model does not imply a consecutive choice process according to a decision tree, as might be inferred from this representation.

Amemiya (1985, pp. 300–3) discusses the nested model more fully, and gives the derivation of probabilities from the distribution (27) for the case of three states of which two form a cluster. He also gives the general formula of the probability model for any number of clusters. For a state s belonging to cluster l, or to the set B_l, this is

$$P_{is} = \frac{\alpha_l \exp - \rho_l^{-1} V_{is} \left\{ \sum_{t \in B_l} \exp - \rho_l^{-1} V_{it} \right\}^{\rho_l - 1}}{\sum_k \alpha_k \left\{ \sum_{t \in B_k} \exp - \rho_k^{-1} V_{it} \right\}^{\rho_k}} \tag{28}$$

As in the standard multinomial logit, the α are normalised by putting $\alpha_1 = 0$ for a reference cluster.

As for estimation, one could consider the classical maximum likelihood

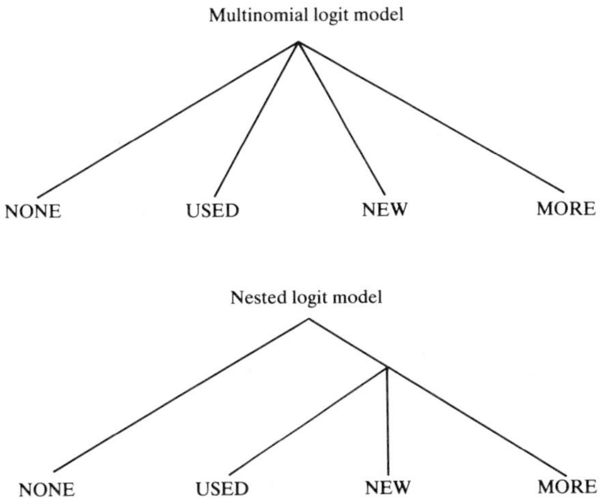

Fig. 4.1 Two logit models of private car ownership.

procedure which is to insert (28) into the loglikelihood function

$$\log L = \sum_i \log L_i = \sum_i \sum_s y_{is} \log P_{is} \tag{29}$$

and maximise the result with respect to all parameters, i.e the α_k, ρ_k, and the parameters that occur in the systematic parts V_{is}. The standard prescription is however a two-step procedure, again proposed by McFadden in his seminal article of 1977. This is first to consider observed choices within each cluster in isolation, and to estimate the relevant logit model for each cluster separately from the logit model.

$$Pr(\text{state } s \text{ at } i \mid s \in B_l) = \frac{\exp V^*_{is}}{\sum_{t \in B_l} \exp V^*_{it}}$$

$$V^*_{is} = -\rho_l^{-1} V_{is} \tag{30}$$

by standard methods. This gives estimates of the coefficients of V^*_{is}, that is of V_{is} multiplied by $-\rho_l^{-1}$. In the second step these values are substituted into (28), and the ensuing expression for (29) is maximised with respect to the α_k and the ρ_k. The main trouble with this procedure is that the variance matrix of the final estimates can not be evaluated by the standard programs which may be used to perform the parameter estimation.

5
Prediction and Fit

5.1 Introduction

On the textbook view, the end result of empirical analysis is a maintained probability model with accepted parameter estimates. But in practice the aim of empirical work is the use of these results in forecasts and policy simulations. For a causal model these exercises involve **conditional prediction**, or prediction for given values of the regressor variables. With a regression equation, this conditional prediction is straightforward.* But with probability models, the issue is not so simple. Let

$$\Pr(\mathbf{y} = \boldsymbol{\iota}_s | \mathbf{x}) = P_s(\mathbf{x}, \boldsymbol{\theta}), \qquad s = 1, 2, \ldots, S \tag{1}$$

be a multinomial probability model, and

$$\mathbf{p}(\mathbf{x}, \boldsymbol{\theta}) \tag{2}$$

the corresponding vector of S probabilities. We also have parameter estimates $\hat{\boldsymbol{\theta}}$ and an estimated variance matrix $\hat{\mathbf{V}}$, short for $\hat{\mathbf{V}}\hat{\boldsymbol{\theta}}$. This model refers to single households, trips, payments or whatever, and it has been estimated from individual observations of the same. The natural prediction at given $\mathbf{x}^\circ$ is therefore

$$\hat{P}_s(\mathbf{x}^\circ) = P_s(\mathbf{x}^\circ, \hat{\boldsymbol{\theta}}) \tag{3}$$

for the probability of a single state s, or

$$\hat{\mathbf{p}}(\mathbf{x}^\circ) = \mathbf{p}(\mathbf{x}^\circ, \hat{\boldsymbol{\theta}}) \tag{4}$$

for the vector of S probabilities. These predictions offer probability statements, not a single value or a **point estimate**, as with regression. They also refer to a single case, a single household, trip or payment. This is so because the analytical model has been designed that way; but that was done to use the full sample information, not because the prediction of individual cases is of interest. On the contrary, the principal purpose of sample surveys and their analysis is to obtain results that can be generalised to larger aggregates.

As a rule, therefore, the practical problem is to predict the **aggregate incidence** of state s, or of all S states, for a given population or group. In this chapter, we deal with this case first, and return afterwards to the prediction of a single observation. The discussion gives rise to several prediction procedures, or **predictors**, which may of course also be applied to the original sample used in

* See for instance Johnston (1984, pp. 42–5).

estimation. This will show whether the method of prediction is any good, but it can also shed some light on the performance of the model in describing the data. This is the link of prediction with considerations of fit, which are explored in the later sections.

Most arguments of this chapter apply to any probability model, but the logit model is the main example we have in mind.

5.2 Prediction of aggregate incidence

Conditional aggregate prediction arises in a forecast of the frequency of certain attributes in a particular population or group, like the future course of national car ownership under certain demographic and economic developments, or the future composition by schooling of manpower demand in a certain region. Conditional aggregate predictions also serve to assess **policy effects**, for example the effect of new tariffs on demand for urban public transport. This is assessed by predicting the modal split of total travel under the new fares, and comparing it with the present situation. The estimated effects of a (small) change of a regressor will in turn give the **aggregate derivative** or **(quasi-) elasticity** for the population under review, which is often more instructive than the point evaluation at the sample mean of these measures of Sections 2.1 and 3.2.

In all these cases we consider a group of M households, individuals, or choices, in brief M independent *experiments* with given regressor vectors $\mathbf{x}_h, h = 1, \ldots, M$. The actual state at a single experiment $\mathbf{y}_h$ is a random variable with mean

$$E\mathbf{y}_h = \mathbf{p}(\mathbf{x}_h, \theta) = \mathbf{p}_h \tag{5}$$

The variance matrix of $\mathbf{y}_h$ is

$$\mathbf{V}\mathbf{y}_h = \bar{\mathbf{p}}_h - \mathbf{p}_h\mathbf{p}_h^{\mathrm{T}} \tag{6}$$

where $\bar{\mathbf{p}}_h$ denotes a diagonal matrix constructed from the vector $\mathbf{p}_h$. The diagonal elements of $\mathbf{V}\mathbf{y}_h$ are $P_{hs}(1 - P_{hs})$ and the off-diagonal covariances are $P_{hs}P_{ht}$.* This variance matrix is singular since the elements of $\mathbf{y}_h$ sum to one; its rows and columns sum to zero.

The aggregate frequencies are given by the vector $\mathbf{v}$

$$\mathbf{v} = \sum_h \mathbf{y}_h \tag{7}$$

A typical element V_s, the **frequency** of state s, has mean and variance

$$EV_s = \sum_h P_s(\mathbf{x}_h, \theta) = \sum_h P_{hs} \tag{8}$$

$$\operatorname{var} V_s = \sum_h P_{hs}(1 - P_{hs}) \tag{9}$$

The **relative frequency** or incidence of state s is

$$f_s = V_s/M, \tag{10}$$

* For the derivation of these convariances see Mood *et al.* (1974), p. 169.

with mean and variance

$$Ef_s = \tilde{P}_s = \frac{1}{M}\sum_h P_{hs} \tag{11}$$

$$\text{var} f_s = \frac{1}{M^2}\sum_h P_{hs}(1 - P_{hs}) \tag{12}$$

Note that the population mean $\tilde{P}_s$ is always defined for a particular aggregate or group, here defined by the M vectors $\mathbf{x}_n$, even if there is no suffix to indicate the fact.

For the vector $\mathbf{v}$ we find

$$E\mathbf{v} = \sum_h \mathbf{p}(\mathbf{x}_h, \boldsymbol{\theta}) = \sum_h \mathbf{p}_h \tag{13}$$

The variance matrix is obtained from (6) by summation over independent observations as

$$\mathbf{V}\mathbf{v} = \sum_h (\bar{\mathbf{p}}_h - \mathbf{p}_h\mathbf{p}_h^{\mathrm{T}}) \tag{14}$$

As a sum of singular matrices, this matrix is of course singular, too.

The vector of relative frequencies **f** is

$$\mathbf{f} = \frac{1}{M}\mathbf{v} \tag{15}$$

with

$$E\mathbf{f} = \tilde{\mathbf{p}} = \frac{1}{M}\sum_h \mathbf{p}(\mathbf{x}_h, \boldsymbol{\theta}) \tag{16}$$

$$\mathbf{V}\mathbf{f} = \frac{1}{M^2}\sum_h (\bar{\mathbf{p}}_h - \mathbf{p}_h\mathbf{p}_h^{\mathrm{T}}) \tag{17}$$

These tedious preliminaries will be needed in what follows. Here they bring out that the relative frequencies which we wish to predict have an intrinsic variation that will never disappear, just like the disturbance variance of a regression model. This is the **sampling variance** of (12) and (17). As several different variances occur in what follows, we recall the principles of their notation at this first opportunity. Var z and $\mathbf{V}\mathbf{z}$ are the variance of z and the variance matrix of $\mathbf{z}$ respectively. Note the distinction between

$$\mathbf{V}\mathbf{z} \qquad \text{and} \qquad \mathbf{V}\hat{\mathbf{z}},$$

which refer to different random variables; the argument is omitted only from $\mathbf{V}\hat{\boldsymbol{\theta}}$, so that $\mathbf{V}$ is always the variance matrix of the maximum likelihood estimates $\hat{\boldsymbol{\theta}}$. Also note the difference between

$$\mathbf{V}\mathbf{z} \qquad \text{and} \qquad \hat{\mathbf{V}}\mathbf{z}$$

which are the true variance matrix and its estimate, obtained as a matter of course by substitution of ML estimates in the expression concerned.

The sampling variances (12) and (17) never disappear altogether, but they do decline with M, and for a sizeable population they become negligible. An element of the summation in (9) cannot exceed 0.25, and neither can the elements of (6). It follows that the elements of (12) can not surpass $0.25/M$, so that the standard deviation of a relative frequency must satisfy

$$\mathrm{sd} f_s < 1/(2\sqrt{M})$$

Since a standard deviation of 0.1 percentage point, or 0.001, surely gives an acceptable precision for a relative frequency, the sampling variation is negligible for M over 250 000, or less to the extent that the probabilities differ from 0.5. Many common aggregates of economic analysis, like the households of a nation, or the trips made in a medium-sized city during a year, easily meet these bounds. But the sampling variation can not be ignored for smaller groups, for instance when we consider the frequency of car ownership (and hence the need for parking space) among the residents of a single apartment building, or the number of aircraft passengers with a reservation that will actually turn up for the flight.

So much for the random aggregate f_s that must be predicted. As in the case of regression, we predict its expected value $\tilde{P}_s$, and we do this by substituting the parameter estimates in (11), or, by (4),

$$\hat{f}_s^1 = \frac{1}{M}\sum_h \hat{P}_{hs} = \frac{1}{M}\sum_h P_s(\mathbf{x}_h, \hat{\boldsymbol{\theta}}) \tag{18}$$

The superscript indicates that this is the first predictor of the population mean $\tilde{P}_s$; others will follow. Since a function of maximum likelihood estimates is itself a ML estimate, (18) is the MLE of $\tilde{P}_s$, and as such it is consistent and asymptotically efficient. Note that 'asymptotic' here refers to the size of the original sample used in estimation; it has nothing to do with the size M of the group to which the estimates are applied.

By (2.59), the asymptotic **estimation variance** of the predictor (18) is given by

$$\mathrm{var}\,\hat{f}_s^1 = \mathbf{d}_s^1 \mathbf{V} \mathbf{d}_s^{1\mathrm{T}} \tag{19}$$

where $\mathbf{d}_s^1$ is the vector of derivatives of $\hat{f}_s^1$ with respect to $\boldsymbol{\theta}$. Note that, by (18), each of these derivatives is a sum of M terms, involving all the $\mathbf{x}_h$. An estimate of this variance is of course obtained by evaluating (19) at the estimated parameter values.

The vector $\mathbf{f}$ is of course predicted in the same way by

$$\hat{\mathbf{f}}^1 = \frac{1}{M}\sum_h \hat{\mathbf{p}}_h = \frac{1}{M}\sum_h \mathbf{p}(\mathbf{x}_h, \hat{\boldsymbol{\theta}}) \tag{20}$$

with estimation variance matrix

$$\mathbf{V}\hat{\mathbf{f}}^1 = \mathbf{D}^1 \mathbf{V} \mathbf{D}^{1\mathrm{T}} \tag{21}$$

where $\mathbf{D}^1$ is the Jacobian matrix of derivatives of $\hat{\mathbf{f}}^1$ with respect to $\boldsymbol{\theta}$.* As before, the elements of $\mathbf{D}^1$ are sums of $\mathbf{M}$ functions of the $\mathbf{x}_h$.

The difference between the sampling variances (12) and (17) on the one hand and the estimation variances (19) and (21) on the other should be clear. The estimation variance of a predictor is due to the use of parameter estimates, and depends on the size and other characteristics of the original sample; the sampling variance is a property of the variable that is being predicted, and it depends on the size of the group to which it refers. Just as with conditional prediction from a linear regression equation, the overall **prediction error** consists of two independent elements, as in

$$\hat{\mathbf{f}}^1 - \mathbf{f} = (\hat{\mathbf{f}}^1 - \tilde{\mathbf{p}}) - (\mathbf{f} - \tilde{\mathbf{p}}) \tag{22}$$

The first term has probability limit zero for an ever-increasing size of the original estimation sample, since $\hat{\mathbf{f}}^1$ is a MLE and hence a consistent estimate of $\tilde{\mathbf{p}}$; the second term has expectation zero, and probability limit zero for an ever-increasing size of the prediction population, by the law of large numbers. For the covariance matrix of the total prediction error we find

$$\mathbf{V}(\hat{\mathbf{f}}^1 - \mathbf{f}) = \mathbf{V}\hat{\mathbf{f}}^1 + \mathbf{V}\mathbf{f} = \mathbf{D}^1\mathbf{V}\mathbf{D}^{1\mathrm{T}} + \frac{1}{M^2}\sum_h (\bar{\mathbf{p}}_h - \mathbf{p}_h\mathbf{p}_h^{\mathrm{T}}) \tag{23}$$

With appropriate changes in the first term, this expression will also hold for the other predictors. As we have seen, M is in practice often so large that the second term can be safely neglected.

For the construction of any aggregate predictor $\hat{\mathbf{f}}$ or $\hat{f}_s$ we need to know the distribution of the regressor variables in the group or population under review. When M is large, this is easier described by their joint density function $g(\mathbf{x}, \zeta)$ than by listing huge numbers of $\mathbf{x}_h$. The expected aggregate incidence of state s is then

$$\tilde{P}_s = \int_x P_s(\mathbf{x}, \boldsymbol{\theta})\, g(\mathbf{x}, \zeta)\, \mathrm{d}\mathbf{x} \tag{24}$$

Since P_s and g are both known functions, it is worth looking for an analytical expression for P_s by integrating $\mathbf{x}$ out, say

$$\tilde{P}_s = f_s(\boldsymbol{\theta}, \zeta) \tag{25}$$

This immediately suggests a second predictor $\hat{f}_s^2$ of $\tilde{P}_s$,

$$\hat{f}_s^2 = f_s(\hat{\boldsymbol{\theta}}, \zeta) \tag{26}$$

which is a typical element of the vector predictor $\hat{\mathbf{f}}^2$. Just like $\hat{\mathbf{f}}^1$, and for the same reasons, this is an MLE of $\tilde{\mathbf{p}}$, and hence a consistent and asymptotically efficient

* With S states and k parameters in $\boldsymbol{\theta}$, $\mathbf{D}^1$ has S rows and k columns; but its rank cannot exceed $(S - 1)$, since the elements of $\mathbf{f}^1$ sum identically to one, and the derivatives sum to zero. $\mathbf{V}\hat{\mathbf{f}}^1$ therefore has at most rank $(S - 1)$, too, and is is singular, as it should be.

predictor. Its asymptotic variance matrix is given by the analogue of (21),

$$\mathbf{V}\hat{\mathbf{f}}^2 = \mathbf{D}^2\mathbf{V}\mathbf{D}^{2\mathrm{T}} \tag{27}$$

The advantages of a neat closed analytical expression for $\hat{\mathbf{f}}^2$ are obvious. The parameters ζ are common characteristics of the population like the mean and variance of the income distribution (or transformations of such characteristics) and their present values are known. For conditional prediction these values are deliberately changed in a given manner, with changes in policy variables translated into changes in ζ. But the effect of regressor variables need no longer be assessed by the roundabout route of a conditional prediction, for aggregate derivatives or elasticities can be obtained at once by differentiating (26) in respect of the elements of ζ that represent changes in the variables under review. The aggregate income elasticity will for instance reflect the effect of a proportional increase in all incomes, that is an increase in mean logincome, with the dispersion of logincome remaining the same. Other definitions are of course possible; but all definitions must be made explicit in terms of ζ.

There are however not many cases where g and P_s mesh to produce a neat analytical expression for (25). I know of no convenient distribution g that accommodates a logit model $P_s(\mathbf{x}, \theta)$. But with P_s a probability function, (24) immediately calls to mind the convolution theorem.* Since this can be applied to the addition of independent Normal variates, there is an easy solution for probit models when the population distribution of their argument is Normal, too. One well-known example is household ownership of durable goods, with P_s a bivariate probit model of Section 2.3 with a single regressor, namely logincome, and g a lognormal income distribution density. In this case, (25) is itself a lognormal distribution function with composite parameters; see Aitchison and Brown (1957, pp. 11, 139), or Lancaster (1979). This is of practical interest, as both the lognormal income distribution and the probit model for durable ownership and other consumer attributes are supported by empirical evidence. McFadden and Reid (1975) use the same technique by assuming a Normal distribution of the linear combination of regressors they use in a probit model of transport mode choice.

Apart from one or two exceptions of this sort, however, the integration of (24) presents intractable analytical problems, certainly when $\mathbf{x}$ has several elements. We may still maintain the density function $f(\mathbf{x}, \zeta)$ and tackle (24) by numerical methods, as Westin (1974) did, but with present computing facilities it is much simpler to represent the distribution of $\mathbf{x}$ in the population by enumeration, though not by a *full* enumeration of all its M elements. Instead of these we use a smaller number of **typical vectors** $\mathbf{x}_h$, with given weights w_h. If these weights are represented by repetition of the vectors concerned, this is equivalent to a synthetic or constructed **prediction set** of m vectors $\mathbf{x}_h$, which together form a small-scale representation of the population. The number of vectors m depends

* For the convolution theorem see Mood *et al.* (1974), p. 186.

on the number of distinct regressor vectors, and on the desired precision of the weighting scheme; it has nothing to do with the population size M.

One way of obtaining such a set is of course to take a random sample from the (sub)population, as when we project car ownership by area on the basis of local samples giving household income, composition, age and so on (but not car ownership). For conditional predictions and policy analyses we adjust the values of one or two regressors, leaving everything else unchanged. The result is a **prediction sample** of m vectors $\mathbf{x}_h$, not to be confused with the **original sample** of n observed vectors $\mathbf{x}_i$ used in estimation. The prediction sample represents the prediction population, which is for instance a future population of households, with changed incomes and a different age composition from today, or the present population with all incomes increased by ten percent, so as to bring out aggregate income effects. Such prediction samples are easily constructed, even on the basis of the original sample, provided this matches the intended population; it should be a random sample in order to represent the present composition of the population correctly.*

For predictions by enumeration over a prediction sample the earlier formulae for $\hat{f}^1$ apply, with the single change that summation takes place over m instead of M elements. For a single attribute s we find, as in (18) and (19),

$$\hat{f}_s^3 = \frac{1}{m}\sum_h \hat{P}_s(\mathbf{x}_h) = \frac{1}{m}\sum_h P_s(x_h, \hat{\boldsymbol{\theta}}) \tag{28}$$

$$\operatorname{var} \hat{f}_s^3 = \mathbf{d}_s^3 \mathbf{V} \mathbf{d}_s^{3\mathrm{T}} \tag{29}$$

and for the entire vector, as in (20) and (21),

$$\hat{\mathbf{f}}^3 = \frac{1}{m}\sum_h \hat{\mathbf{p}}_h = \frac{1}{m}\sum_h \mathbf{p}(\mathbf{x}_h, \hat{\boldsymbol{\theta}}) \tag{30}$$

$$\mathbf{V}\hat{\mathbf{f}}^3 = \mathbf{D}^3 \mathbf{V} \mathbf{D}^{3\mathrm{T}} \tag{31}$$

with obvious modifications in the definition of $\mathbf{d}_s^3$ and $\mathbf{D}^3$.

The expressions (28) and (30) present no problems. As for (29) and (31), note once more that the vector or matrix of derivatives $\mathbf{d}_s^3$ and $\mathbf{D}^3$ consist of sums over the m elements of the prediction set, evaluated at the prediction regressor vectors $\mathbf{x}_h$, while $\mathbf{V}$ is a sum of n elements defined for the observed regressor vectors $\mathbf{x}_i$ of the original sample. If the prediction sample is constructed by modifying the original sample, the number will be the same, but the prediction vectors $\mathbf{x}_h$ will still differ in one or more elements from the observed vectors $\mathbf{x}_i$.

This completes the discussion of predictors of aggregate (relative) frequencies. We have distinguished three predictors by superscripts, but conceptually they are the same, and the differences lie only in the method of calculation. This is different in the next section.

* By the argument of Section 2.4, the original sample need not be random for the purpose of estimation, provided there is no endogenous selection.

5.3 Prediction of individual outcomes

Predicting the state that will obtain at a given regressor vector $\mathbf{x}^\circ$ is tantamount to predicting the outcome of a single statistical experiment like the throw of a die, and almost equally futile; but it can serve as a basis for aggregate predictions. The major difficulty of the individual prediction is that **admissible predictors** are limited to values that can in fact occur. Take the simple case of a bivariate probability model for a single household attribute, car ownership, with parameters that are known or estimated with any desired precision. For a household with a given vector $\mathbf{x}^\circ$ let the probability of car ownership be 0.75. This is also the expected value of the dependent (0,1) variable $Y|\mathbf{x}^\circ$, but it is not an admissible prediction since Y can never take this value. For an admissible predictor we need a decision rule which attaches 0 or 1 to Y on the basis of the probability of these values.

In the example given, the natural choice is 1, since 0.75 exceeds 0.5. This is the **maximum probability rule** 'predict the most probable state'. The rule can also be applied to a probability model with more states, and it ensures the largest probability of a correct prediction. If the loss function associated with wrong predictions is symmetrical in respect of all states, it is an optimal decision rule. A major drawback of the rule is however that its outcome is sensitive to the number of alternative states. If we wish to predict the ownership of more than one car, it can make a considerable difference whether this state is contrasted to two alternatives (no car, one car) or to three (no car, one used car, one new car). The probability of multiple car ownership remains the same, but the chance that it is the largest probability depends on the number (and nature) of the alternatives considered.

A second objection to the maximum probability rule is that it almost always leads to severely biased results in repeated predictions under identical conditions. These will show a 100% incidence of one state and zero for the others, and the corresponding aggregate predictor is neither unbiased nor consistent for the expected frequency. Similarly, if the rule is applied to the elements of a prediction sample with varying $\mathbf{x}_h$, the sum of the results will only by chance produce an unbiased or consistent prediction of the expected aggregate frequency. It is easy to think of a case where the probability of one state among S is the largest for all sample observations, even though on average it is not much larger than $1/S$, and varies considerably from one observation to another. The maximum probability rule will then attach $Y = 1$ to all observations, and predict 100% as the relative frequency of the state, though its expected incidence is much smaller. Conversely the maximum probability rule underestimates the incidence of rare attributes, such as multiple car ownership, rare diseases, or trips ending in fatal collisions. It predicts that rare events never occur, while in fact they happen regularly.*

*This is apparently overlooked by Fomby *et. al.* (1984, p. 352), who say that the maximum probability rule correctly predicts the expected aggregate frequency.

Against the last objection it can be argued thet there is no point in judging individual predictors by their performance in generating aggregate predictions, since we have already found several perfectly satisfactory aggregate predictors which make no use of individual predictions. But there is at least one case with a genuine need for acceptable aggregate predictions that are based on admissible individual predictions, namely when the probability model is part of a wider **micro simulation model**. In such a model, the prediction sample or **simulation set** of m elements that provides a small-scale image of the population is used to carry many interdependent dynamic processes. The standard example is the demographic development of a human population over a longer period. This involves the birth, ageing, marriage, parenthood and death of single individuals. These processes cannot be accurately represented by average birth rates, marriage rates and so on, and we must simulate individual life histories instead. In the same way, the working of the economic system can be represented by making representative sets of households, individuals, and firms act out their interdependent behaviour under various conditions.* If the probability model is embedded in such a wider model, the prediction of aggregate incidence is not good enough. A given car ownership rate, for instance, must be specified by indicating which individual households have cars, for in the next step of the simulation these cars generate trips and mileage, affect other expenditure, in short set off an entire train of microeconomic consequences.

The solution to this problem is the **random simulation rule** which consists in the random selection of states with the appropriate (estimated) probabilities. A simple method of doing this is to identify the estimated probabilities with consecutive intervals of the (0,1) interval, and then to draw a random number with uniform distribution over this interval to select a state. The rule leads at the same time to admissible random predictions and to an acceptable prediction of the aggregate incidence.

By this rule, the prediction of $\mathbf{y}|\mathbf{x}_h$ is the random outcome of the accepted probability model with estimated parameter vector $\hat{\boldsymbol{\theta}}$. Thus the individual predictor $\hat{\mathbf{y}}_h$ is a random variable with

$$\Pr(\hat{\mathbf{y}}_h = \mathbf{\iota}_s) = P_s(\mathbf{x}_h, \hat{\boldsymbol{\theta}}) = \hat{P}_s(\mathbf{x}_h) \tag{32}$$

and expected value

$$E\hat{\mathbf{y}}_h = \hat{\mathbf{p}}(\mathbf{x}_h) \tag{33}$$

The mean of the m random vectors $\hat{\mathbf{y}}_h$ in the simulation set predicts aggregate incidence by

$$\hat{\mathbf{f}}^4 = \frac{1}{m}\sum_h \hat{\mathbf{y}}_h \tag{34}$$

* See the seminal work in this area by Orcutt *et al.* (1961) or a later survey by Bergmann *et al.* (1980).

Its expectation is

$$E\hat{\mathbf{f}}^4 = \frac{1}{m}\sum_h \hat{\mathbf{p}}(\mathbf{x}_h) = \frac{1}{m}\sum_h \hat{\mathbf{p}}_h \tag{35}$$

By the construction of the simulation set and the consistency of $\hat{\mathbf{p}}(\mathbf{x}_h)$, this should be a consistent prediction of the true expected aggregate incidence $\tilde{\mathbf{p}}$.

As in Section 5.2 we must distinguish between the **sampling variance** and the **estimation variance** of this predictor. For the sampling variance we can use the same expression as before, in (17), with m instead of M and $\hat{\mathbf{p}}_h$ instead of $\mathbf{p}_h$, viz.

$$\mathbf{V}\hat{\mathbf{f}}^4 = \frac{1}{m^2}\sum_h (\bar{\hat{\mathbf{p}}}_h - \hat{\mathbf{p}}_h\hat{\mathbf{p}}_h^{\mathrm{T}}) \tag{36}$$

Can this variance be ignored on the same grounds as before? At first sight this depends on the value of m. This is far smaller than M, for the whole point of a simulation set is that it contains far less elements than the population it describes. m is set by the need for a fair representation of the joint variation of the elements of $\mathbf{x}_h$ in the population; it is usually of the order of a thousand or so, as opposed to many millions of M. But if the simulation were an isolated exercise, exclusively designed to estimate $\tilde{\mathbf{p}}$, the number of independent observations could be increased at will to any multiple of m by repeating the entire simulation and hence the random drawings at each $\mathbf{x}_h$, and this would solve the problem. As we have indicated above, however, the present predictor makes sense only in the context of the simulation of a much wider model. It follows that there is no point in assessing the sampling variance matrix (36) of $\hat{\mathbf{f}}^4$ alone, nor in repeating the calculation of this random vector by itself, in isolation, to reduce its sampling variance. If we wish to evaluate sampling variance, or to reduce it by increasing the number of independent individual simulations, the simulation of the entire model should be repeated.

As for the **estimation variance** of $\hat{\mathbf{f}}^4$, this would be given as before by an expression like

$$\mathbf{V}\hat{\mathbf{f}}^4 = \mathbf{D}^4\mathbf{V}\mathbf{D}^{4\mathrm{T}} \tag{37}$$

In the present case, however, there is no way of determining the matrix $\mathbf{D}^4$ of derivatives of the **random** vector $\hat{\mathbf{f}}^4$ in respect of the elements of θ. We therefore cannot determine this expression or evaluate its estimated value. Again, there is much more interest in the estimation variance of the outcome of the larger simulation of which $\hat{\mathbf{f}}^4$ is part than in the estimation variance of this predictor alone. Unfortunately, these outcomes are even less amenable to the analytical determination of their derivatives in respect of the parameters. A simulation model has been designed since the process is too complex for a model that can be solved and studied by analytical methods, and it is impossible to obtain the estimation variance of its outcome by a formula like (37). The best one can do is to subject the average outcome of repeated simulation runs (so as to reduce sampling variance) to a **sensitivity analysis** by repeating the entire exercise with small changes in the parameter estimates, taking one parameter at a time.

5.4 Measures of fit based on individual observations

Take a linear regression model

$$Y_i = \mathbf{x}_i^{\mathrm{T}}\boldsymbol{\beta} + \varepsilon_i \tag{38}$$

with n observations and k parameters in $\boldsymbol{\beta}$. An individual **residual** is

$$e_i = Y_i - \mathbf{x}_i^{\mathrm{T}}\hat{\boldsymbol{\beta}} \tag{39}$$

and the **total** and **residual sum of squares** are

$$TSS = \sum_i (Y_i - \bar{Y})^2 \tag{40}$$

$$RSS = \sum_i e_i^2 \tag{41}$$

These serve for three conventional measures of fit or performance of the estimated model, namely

$$s^2 = RSS/(n-k) \tag{42}$$

which is an estimate of the disturbance variance σ^2,

$$R^2 = 1 - RSS/TSS \tag{43}$$

and

$$F = \{R^2/(1-R^2)\}\{(n-k)/\mathrm{k}\} \tag{44}$$

These measures are variously invoked to compare different specifications, to illustrate that the fitted model is satisfactory, and to prove that it contributes to the explanation of the variable under review. Ideally, σ^2 (and hence s^2) should be small; R^2 should be close to unity; and (with Normal ε_i) F should be highly significant in a $F(n-k), k$ distribution. The separate residuals are moreover used in several other tests, and their inspection can point to errors and omissions in the model specification and indicate outliers among the observations.

There is a universal desire for similar measures, permitting similar judgements, for the logit model and for probability models in general. Apart from the significance test of the overall model, this wish cannot be fulfilled, for these models have no comparable residuals and no disturbance variance σ^2.

This is not to say that it is impossible to define residuals. In the bivariate case (which is the only case studied in the literature), we have a single (0,1) variable Y_i, with a single P_i and $Q_i = 1 - \mathrm{P}_i$. a natural definition of a scalar residual is then

$$e_i = Y_i - \hat{P}_i \tag{45}$$

with a corresponding residual sum of squares

$$RSS = \sum_i (Y_i - \hat{P}_i)^2 \tag{46}$$

The variance of e_i is $\hat{P}_i\hat{Q}_i$, and for the sum of squared **standardised** residuals we find

$$RSS^* = \sum_i (Y_i - \hat{P}_i)^2/\hat{P}_i\hat{Q}_i \tag{47}$$

This is the sum of squares of n independent random variables with unit variance. Although they are not Normal, it is sometimes suggested in the literature that RSS^* is asymptotically chi square distributed with $n - k$ degrees of freedom, with k the number of fitted parameters; see e.g. Pregibon (1981, p. 709) or Kay and Little (1986, p. 21). This appears to be based on a generalisation of the argument for grouped data, which we shall set out in the next section.

In the multinomial case, however, there is no such immediate scalar measure of the residual deviation. We recall that in the last section we failed to find a single, unique predictor for the individual discrete outcome $\mathbf{y}_h$. This difficulty carries over to the prediction of individual observations of the original sample, and hence to residuals. In a multinomial probability model, the nearest thing to a predicted sample value is

$$\hat{P}_{iy} = \mathbf{y}_i^{\mathrm{T}}\hat{\mathbf{p}}_i \tag{48}$$

As $\mathbf{y}_i$ has 1 in one position and zeros elsewhere, this is the estimated probability of the observed event at observation i. In the subscript of $\hat{P}_{iy}$ we use y as a shorthand notation for $s(i)$, that is the state that actually obtains at the ith observation. Note that by its definition of (2.50) the estimated loglikelihood $\log \hat{L}_i$ is

$$\log L_i(\hat{\theta}) = \sum_s Y_{is} \log \hat{P}_{is} = \log \hat{P}_{iy} \tag{49}$$

so that the sample maximum loglikelihood is

$$\log L(\hat{\theta}) = \sum_i \log L_i(\hat{\theta}) = \sum_i \log \hat{P}_{iy} \tag{50}$$

If $\hat{P}_{iy}$ is the nearest thing to a prediction of $\mathbf{y}_i$, the nearest thing to a multinomial residual is

$$e_i^{\circ} = 1 - \hat{P}_{iy} \tag{51}$$

where we take the deviation from the ideal case of a perfectly certain (and correct) prediction. This residual has some odd features – it is always positive, for instance – but in the bivariate case it is equal to the absolute value of e_i of (45), and hence yields the same RSS.

Even if we have residuals, however, they can not be used for an estimate of the variance of unexplained disturbances, because there is no such thing in probability models. This is why we managed to standardise the residuals in (47) without the benefit of σ^2. It also explains why there are no valid analogues to the linear regression measures. It is true that two derivations of the logit model make use of a systematic function of regressor variables with an additive random term, which is highly suggestive; but we must recall that in both cases the disturbance variance is confounded with the systematic component, and can not be identified as a separate parameter.

The *first* instance is the threshold model for the bivariate logit in Sections 2.2 and 2.3. The disturbance has a logistic distribution with zero mean, any nonzero mean being absorbed into the intercept; its standard deviation is a scale parameter that is likewise absorbed in the reaction coefficients. It is therefore not identified, and even if it were identified by somehow fixing the reaction coefficients it would show up in the slope of the logit curve, not in a distinct measure of fit.* The *second* case is the discrete choice model for the multinomial logit of Section 3.3. The underlying independent disturbances of the random utilities have a Type I extreme value distribution with a common nonzero mean and a common variance—see (3.42) and (3.43). But this common standard deviation is again unidentified and absorbed into the slope coefficients, and again it does not show up in a separate sample statistic.

The conclusion is that there is no point in the search for an analogue to the residual variance of linear regression. A much better starting point is the sample maximum loglikelihood $\log L(\hat{\boldsymbol{\theta}})$ of (50),

$$\log L(\hat{\boldsymbol{\theta}}) = \sum_i \log \hat{P}_{iy}$$

The probabilities $\hat{P}_{iy}$ lie between zero and 1; for a perfect fit $\hat{P}_{iy}$ should be as close to 1 as possible, with the probability of all other states close to zero. Hence $\log L(\hat{\boldsymbol{\theta}})$ is always negative, and the closer to zero it is, the better the fit. At the other end of the scale we may define **naive models**, and consider $\log L(\mathbf{0})$, with all coefficients zero and the probabilities of all states equal to $1/S$ for all i, or $\log L(\hat{\boldsymbol{\beta}}_0)$ with only a single intercept estimated for each state. As was shown in Section 3.6, equation (3.69), the probabilities of this **base line model** are equal to the sample frequencies. This seems to provide a better standard than the first model, which is exceedingly simplistic.

Thus $\log L(\hat{\boldsymbol{\theta}})$ is, as it were, suspended between 0 and the one hand and the base line likelihood on the other, or

$$\log L(\hat{\boldsymbol{\beta}}_0) < \log \mathrm{L}(\hat{\boldsymbol{\theta}}) < 0 \tag{52}$$

We examine the relative position of $\log L(\boldsymbol{\theta})$ to both neighbours in turn. First, the distance from $\log L(\hat{\boldsymbol{\beta}}_0)$ can be used to test for the explanatory power of the given model over the base line model by a LR test, as was shown in eq. (2.70) and eq. (3.70)†. The substance (but not the form!) of this test closely resembles the F test

* The same holds of course for the probit model of Section 2.3.

† It does not seem much use to define a pseudo-R^2 or a rho square measure $1 - \log L(\hat{\boldsymbol{\theta}})/\log L(\hat{\boldsymbol{\beta}}_0)$ which is then used in a fashion similar to R^2. For a different opinion, see Judge *et al.* (1980), p. 602, or Ben-Akiva and Lerman (1987), p. 167.

for the significance of a regression, based on (44). In both cases we almost invariably find a significant result, as only a single regressor need contribute to the explanation of the observed variation in Y to achieve this.

At the other side of (52), some authors suggest a similar LR test of the estimated model against the zero loglikelihood of a perfect model by defining the **deviance**

$$D = -2\log L(\hat{\boldsymbol{\theta}}) \tag{53}$$

This is then treated as an LR test statistic, (asymptotically) chi square distributed with $(n - k)$ degrees of freedom; see McCullagh and Nelder (1983), Pregibon (1981, p. 709), and Kay and Little (1986, p. 20). In practice, this measure always refers to a bivariate model, and its interpretation presumes that the perfect model with loglikelihood zero, which correctly attributes probabilities one and zero to all observations, has n parameters. It is however doubtful whether we can indeed formulate such a model within which the present model is nested.*

With these reservations, $\log L(\hat{\boldsymbol{\theta}})$ is a natural measure of fit, and it can be used intuitively for comparisons between different models fitted to the same data set, even if they are not nested, and also for comparisons between the same model fitted to different data sets. Observe, however, that it varies in proportion with the sample size; to correct for this we should use the mean sample loglikelihood

$$\log L(\hat{\boldsymbol{\theta}})/n \tag{54}$$

for comparisons between data sets. Note that by (50)

$$\bar{\hat{P}}_y = \exp(\log L(\hat{\boldsymbol{\theta}})/n) \tag{55}$$

is the geometric sample mean of the estimated probabilities of observed events $\hat{P}_{iy}$.

Apart from its variation with n, $\log L(\hat{\boldsymbol{\theta}})$ also increases with the number of fitted parameters k. This factor is taken into account in the **Akaike information criterion (AIC)** defined as

$$AIC = -2/n(\log L(\hat{\boldsymbol{\theta}}) - k) \tag{56}$$

This criterion was derived by its author from the consideration of a loss function based on the comparison of the maintained model with a large number of supposedly inferior alternative models (Akaike, 1973). It has been designed to compare the performance of different models on different data sets: the lower the value of AIC, the better the fit.

We illustrate these various measures for two earlier analyses, viz. the multinomial model of car ownership of Section 3.7 and the conditional logit analysis of modes of payment of Section 4.3. Table 5.1 summarises the main characteristics of these entirely different analyses.

* But see the saturated model for grouped data in the next section.

Table 5.1 Goodness of fit statistics of two earlier analyses.

	Car ownership*	Mode of payment†
Number of observations n	2820	2161
number of estimated parameters k	18	5
$\log L(\hat{\beta})$ maximum loglikelihood of fitted model	−2847.90	−816.55
$\log L(\hat{\beta}_0)$ maximum loglikelihood of base-line model	−3528.37	−1052.68
LR test statistic	1360.94	472.26
Mean probability $\bar{P}_y$ of eq. (55)	0.364	0.685
AIC of eq. (56)	2.490	0.760

* See Table 3.1, lines 0 and 5.
† See Table 4.3, model C.

Both analyses distinguish four states, but the distribution of the sample frequencies differ, and this is reflected in the base-line loglikelihood as well as in the overall level of all other loglikelihoods. It is easy to see that the base-line loglikelihood as given in (3.70)

$$\log L^\circ = \sum_s n_s \log n_s - n \log n \tag{57}$$

has the same (unattainable) *maximum* as any loglikelihood, namely zero. It approaches this value as the sample observations are more and more concentrated in a single state, with relative frequency close to 1, while the frequencies of the other states go to zero. In contrast, the *minimum* value of (57) obtains when all states have the same relative frequency $1/S$. In the present examples this is when the sample frequency of every state is 0.25, and

$$\text{minimum} \log L^\circ = n \log 0.25$$

or −3909.35 for the car ownership sample and −2959.78 for the mode of payment observations. Observe in Table 5.1 that for the payment sample the base-line loglikelihood is much farther from its minimum, and closer to the ideal, than for the car ownership sample, simply because a single state (the currency mode) is so highly dominant.

We also see from Table 5.1 that both analyses are highly significant by the overall LR statistic. The geometric mean probability is much higher, and the AIC is much lower (and therefore better) for mode of payment than for car ownership. But we have just seen that this better performance is at least in part due to a better starting position of the observed sample.

A striking result is that the estimated probabilities of the observed events fall so far short of the ideal value of 1, as is illustrated by the (geometric) sample means over all observations, $\hat{P}_y$ of (55).

Finally there is the question of the fit to individual observations, addressed in linear regression studies by inspection of the residuals. Here we may use the individual values of $\hat{P}_{iy}$ for this end. Their inspection brings very clearly to light how poor the fit of the probability model is at the individual level. The analysis of car ownership of Section 3.8 was quite successful in that it yields sensible results and significant coefficients. Yet if we examine the value of $\hat{P}_{iy}$ for all 2820 observations, we find the frequency distribution of Fig. 5.1.

The bulk of the predicted probabilities of observed events lies between 0.1 and 0.6 and there are few values in the upper deciles, with only 3% exceeding 0.9. The fit, as illustrated by the distribution of predicted probabilities, moreover, varies between states, as Fig. 5.2 shows. The results are best for the car ownership categories NONE and USED; the former at least has some probabilities in the

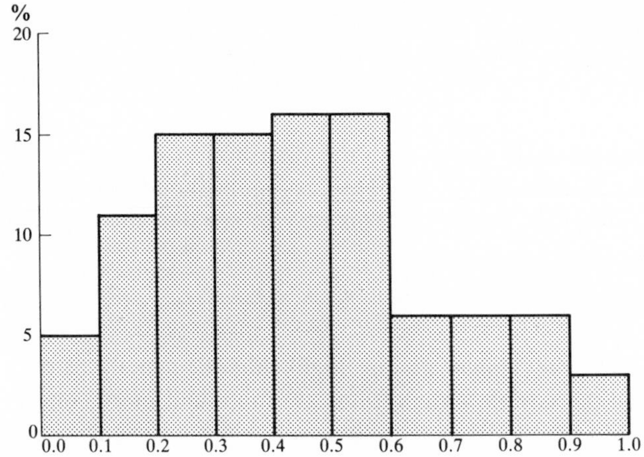

Fig. 5.1 Frequency distribution of predicted probabilities of the observed state (car ownership analysis of Table 2.8).

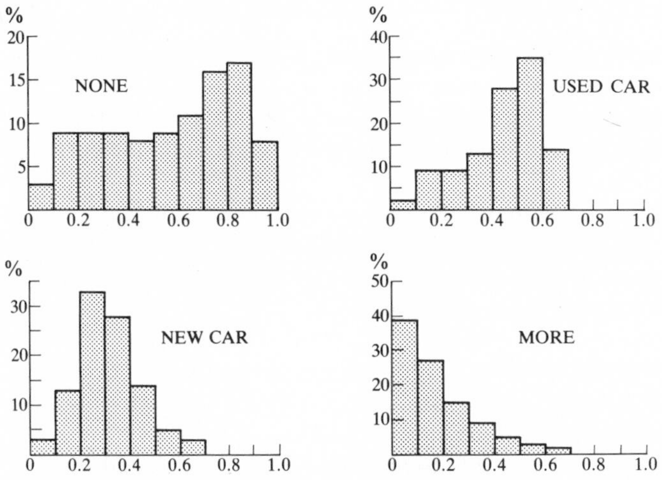

Fig. 5.2 Frequency distribution of predicted probabilities of the observed state, by state.

upper reaches, and the second has a mode between 0.5 and 0.6, but nothing beyond 0.7. NEW is predicted very badly, with most probabilities between 0.2 and 0.4, and MORE is just terrible, with almost 40% of the probabilities below 0.1. The bad result for this last category is probably due to the fact that MORE is a rare state, which holds for only 6% of the sample. In terms of the overall loglikelihood which one wishes to maximise, adjustments of the parameters that improve the prediction of such a rare state are far less profitable than improvements for the larger categories.

The utter failure of the model to predict individual events, even in the sample used in estimation, may shock the reader. Yet these results are by no means exceptional. On the face of it, the car ownership analysis we use as an illustration was quite successful. We also wish to point out that a regression analysis of, say, expenditure on meat, will equally yield very large residuals if we consider individual households, not some aggregate that has been smoothed by the law of large numbers.*

It is an interesting question whether these findings reflect on the passing inadequacy of the present models, or whether we can not hope for a better prediction of individual behaviour by the nature of things.

5.5 Measures of fit for grouped observations

For grouped observations, the principal objection to test or measures of goodness of fit disappears, since the observed data consists of the *frequencies* of the S states in the homogeneous cells of some multidimensional classification of the sample by the regressor variables. The observed data themselves are *aggregates*, provided the cell numbers are not too small; with some goodness of fit tests there are explicit standards for the minimum frequency.

We briefly recall the nature and notation of grouped observations from Section 2.6. Such data arise when all regressor variables are measured in classes or strata, either by their nature, as in the case of urbanisation, or by the design of the questionnaire or the subsequent coding of the answers, as in the case of income classes. If *all* regressor variables are of this **categorical** type, their joint sample distribution is fully described by the corresponding cross tabulation of the individual observations. Empty cells, which are bound to occur in such a classification, are ignored; the classification has J non-empty cells with index j, and there are n_j observations in each. The regressor vectors are $\mathbf{x}_j$; the values of these regressors are set by conventional scales, as in the case of urbanisation, or by the mid-point of the relevant class, as with income classes. The sample information is completed by the frequencies of the S states s in each cell, given by the numbers n_{js}, subject to

$$\sum_s n_{js} = n_j \tag{58}$$

* See Cramer (1969), p. 78 for an illustration.

The probability model assigns probabilities to each state s in cell j according to

$$P_{js} = P_s(\mathbf{x}_j, \boldsymbol{\theta}) \tag{59}$$

As we have seen in Sections 2.6 and 3.5, estimation proceeds as if the n_j observations of cell j constitute repeated observations at a single regressor vector $\mathbf{x}_j$. This approach ignores all within-cell variation, but then so does the arrangement of the sample data.*

As before, we have parameter estimates $\hat{\boldsymbol{\theta}}$, and predictions of the probabilities (59)

$$\hat{P}_{js} = p_s(\mathbf{x}_j, \hat{\boldsymbol{\theta}}) \tag{60}$$

as well as predicted frequencies

$$\hat{n}_{js} = n_j \hat{P}_{js} \tag{61}$$

The probabilities correspond to the observed relative frequencies

$$f_{js} = n_{js}/n_j \tag{62}$$

So much for notation. The classical Pearson test statistic for the null hypothesis that the observed frequencies n_{js} constitute a sample from the distribution with probabilities P_{js} is

$$\text{chi}_j^2 = \sum_s \frac{(n_{js} - \hat{n}_{js})^2}{\hat{n}_{js}} \tag{63}$$

which has a chi square distribution, provided the numbers are not too small; the standard prescription is that the $\hat{n}_{js}$ must not be smaller than 5.† If the P_{js} have been established independently from the observed sample, this has $S - 1$ degrees of freedom; in the other cases we must deduct the number of degrees used up in estimation or fitting.

In the present case we add these independent statistics over all cells to obtain

$$\text{chi}^2 = \sum_j \sum_s \frac{(n_{js} - \hat{n}_{js})^2}{\hat{n}_{js}} \tag{64}$$

which is of course again chi square distributed under the null hypothesis that the observed sample comes from the assumed distribution. It is this quantity which was used as the criterion function for estimating $\boldsymbol{\theta}$ in a bivariate logit model in Section 2.6. Its proper use, however, is in testing the goodness of fit of the estimated probability distribution. When $\hat{\boldsymbol{\theta}}$ is a consistent estimate, like the maximum likelihood estimate, the test applies asymptotically provided we deduct further degrees of freedom for the number of parameters, say k, and (64) has $J \times (S - 1) - k$ degrees of freedom in all.

* The above formulation strongly suggests that the probability model is a standard multinomial logit, but insofar as the grouped data can be treated as repeated observations, the field can be extended to conditional or nested logit models, or indeed to any probability model whatsoever.

† See Mood *et al.* (1974), pp. 442–8.

With grouped observations, another test of the goodness of fit can be obtained from the likelihood ratio test. We regard the fitted model as a restricted variant of a **saturated model** that provides a perfect fit in the sense that the predicted probabilities for each cell equal the observed frequencies; see Bishop *et al.* (1975), pp. 125–6. In this model we put

$$\hat{P}^*_{js} = f_{js} \qquad \text{for all } j \text{ and } s. \tag{65}$$

We thus 'estimate' $J \times (S - 1)$ parameters in the $\hat{P}^*_{js}$ (not to be confused with the model $\hat{P}_{js}$); all the available degrees of freedom are used up in the process. The maximum loglikelihood is

$$\log L^* = \sum_j \sum_s n_{js} \log f_{js} = \sum_j \sum_s n_{js} \log n_{js} - \sum_j n_j \log n_j \tag{66}$$

and this is indeed a maximum maximorum. With a little ingenuity it must be possible to represent the fitted model as a restricted version of this saturated model, and it follows that the likelihood ratio test statistic is

$$LR(s) = 2 \sum_j \sum_s (n_{js} \log f_{js} - n_{js} \log \hat{P}_{js}) \tag{67}$$

This is again chi square distributed with $J \times (S - 1) - k$ degrees of freedom. For grouped data we may thus distinguish three values of $\log L$ with $(S - 1)$, k, and $J \times (S - 1)$ fitted parameters respectively, namely the base-like model, with the $\log L$ of (3.70), the analytical probability model under consideration, and the saturated model. Always omitting the common combinatorial constant, these likelihoods are, in ascending order,

$$\sum_s n_s \log n_s - n \log n \tag{68a}$$

$$\sum_j \sum_s n_{js} \log \hat{P}_{js} \tag{68b}$$

$$\sum_j \sum_s n_{js} \log f_{js} \tag{68c}$$

A comparison of the first and the second term gives the standard overall likelihood ratio test, which tests whether the model contributes significantly to an explanation of the observed frequencies at all. A comparison of the second and the third term gives the likelihood ratio test of (67), which tests for the agreement between the model and the observed frequencies.*

Both goodness of fit tests (64) and (67) have the same asymptotic distribution, but they are not identical and they may well differ in finite samples. We can express both statistics in terms of the agreement between relative frequencies and estimated probabilities within each cell of the grouped data. The chi square

* A total likelihood ratio based on the first and the third term would test whether the classification of data into the cells of the multidimensional classification by the regressor variables is at all relevant to the incidence of the S states under review, regardless of the specification of a model.

statistic (64) is rewritten as

$$\sum_j \sum_s n_j \frac{(f_{js} - \hat{P}_{js})^2}{\hat{P}_{js}} \tag{69}$$

and the likelihood ratio (67) as

$$\sum_j \sum_s n_{js} \log (f_{js}/\hat{P}_{js})^2 \tag{70}$$

Let us examine the behaviour of these statistics. If the discrepancies between frequencies and probabilities were constant, they would both increase linearly with the overall sample size n, with the n_j varying in proportion. But in fact this increase will be kept in check by a reduction of the discrepancies: the $\hat{P}_{js}$ converge to the true P_{js} since they are consistent estimates, and the f_{js} do so because of the law of large numbers. The differences in (69) therefore converge to zero, and the ratios in (70) to unity.

Table 5.2 Performance tests of car ownership analysis by income class (grouped data) of Table 2.4.

Test	Null	D.f.	Value
Chi square of eq. (64)	Model is true	$5-2=3$	2.09
LR(1), eq. (68a–68b)	Income does not explain ownership	$2-1=1$	17.49**
LR(2), eq. (68b–68c)	Income explains ownership fully	$5-2=3$	5.7
Base-line model	$\log L(\beta_0) = -1839.63$		
Estimated model	$\log L(\hat{\beta}) = -1830.88$		
Saturated model	$\log L^* = -1828.04$		

We illustrate these various statistics for the fit of a probability model to grouped data in Table 5.2 for the only example of such an analysis we have, viz. the bivariate car ownership analysis of Section 2.6, with income the sole regressor and five income classes the J cells. At the top of the table we find that the goodness of fit statistic (64) is not significant, and further on that the fitted model is an acceptable simplification of the saturated model by the likelihood ratio statistic of (68b, 68c). Again the other likelihood ratio test, based on (68a, 68b) is significant, which shows that income does contribute to an explanation of car ownership. These results illustrate that the tests are not very strict. We find quite acceptable results, while the income class analysis of Section 2.6 was earlier found to be pretty poor. The reason is that the entire analysis is relative to the classification by five income classes, which is itself a meagre representation of the variation in car ownership. In this much simplified classification there is little variation in ownership between classes (see Table 2.3), and this leads to a small interval between the baseline model and the saturated model. Yet there is a definite relation of ownership frequency to income.

In practice, all these asymptotically valid tests cause trouble when they are applied to very large samples, say census data. If the cell numbers n_j are a few thousand or so, the observed relative frequencies must be very close to the estimated probabilities to fall within the limits of sampling variation. In practice, both goodness of fit tests will therefore produce highly significant test results for such large samples, even though the actual agreement between the f_{js} and $\hat{P}_{js}$ looks reasonable enough. Many experienced analysts hold that the tests are too strict, since they prescribe the rejection of what looks like an acceptable result. With large samples, significant values of the test statistics are therefore rarely taken seriously. The reason is that the tests allow for sampling variation only, and do not leave any room for the approximate nature of the model specification. Under the null hypothesis, the probability model is a true and completely adequate description of the sample experiment, and with increasing sample size predictions must converge to the prescribed probabilities without any discrepancies. This stands in contrast to the regression model, where disturbance are an irreducible feature of any predictions, however large the sample may be. This brings us back once more to the argument of Section 5.4 that probability models have no disturbance term as an independent source of nuisance variation, and that there is hence no equivalent of R^2.

References

Adam, D., 1958. *Les Réactions du Consommateur devant les Prix*. Paris: Sedes.

Aitchison, J. and J. A. C. Brown, 1957. *The Lognormal Distribution*. Cambridge: Cambridge University Press.

Akaike, H., 1973. 'Information theory and an extension of the Maximum Likelihood principle,' in B. N. Petrov and F. Csaki (eds), *Second International Symposium on information theory*. Budapest: Akademia.

Amemiya, T., 1981. 'Qualitative response models: a survey,' *Journal of Economic Literature* **19,** 1483–1536.

Amemiya, T., 1985. *Advanced Econometrics*. Cambridge, Mass.: Harvard University Press.

Amemiya, T. and Q. H. Vuong, 1987. 'A comparison of two consistent estimators in the choice-based sampling qualitative response model,' *Econometrica* **55,** 699–702.

Ben-Akiva, M. and S. R. Lerman, 1987. *Discrete Choice Analysis: Theory and Application to Travel Demand*. Cambridge, Mass.: MIT Press.

Bergmann, B., G. Eliasson and G. Orcutt, 1980. *Micro Simulation—Models, Methods and Applications*. Stockholm: Almquist and Wiksell.

Berkson, J., 1944. 'Application of the logistic function to bio-assay,' *Journal of the American Statistical Association* **39,** 357–65.

Berkson, J., 1951. 'Why I prefer logits to probits,' *Biometrics* **7,** 327–39.

Berkson, J., 1953. 'A statistically precise and relatively simple method of estimating the bio-assay with quantal response based on the logistic function,' *Journal of the American Statistical Association* **48,** 565–99.

Berkson, J., 1980. 'Minimum Chi-square, not Maximum Likelihood!,' *Annals of Mathematical Statistics* **8,** 457–87.

Bishop, Y. M. M., S. E. Fienberg and P. W. Holland, 1975. *Discrete Multivariate Analysis*. Cambridge, Mass.: MIT Press.

Bliss, C. I., 1934. 'The method of probits,' *Science* **79,** 39–9, 409–10.

Cosslett, S. R., 1977. 'Efficient estimation of discrete choice models,' in C. F. Manski and D. McFadden (eds), *Structural Analysis of Discrete Data with Econometric Applications*. Cambridge, Mass.: MIT Press.

Cosslett, S. R., 1981. 'Maximum likelihood estimator for choice-based samples,' *Econometrica* **49,** 1289–1315.

Cramer, J. S., 1969. *Empirical Econometrics*. Amsterdam: North Holland.

Cramer, J. S., 1986a, *Econometric Applications of Maximum Likelihood Methods*. Cambridge: Cambridge University Press.

Cramer, J. S., 1986b. 'Estimation of probability models from income class data,' *Statistica Neerlandica* **40,** 237–50.

Daganzo, C., 1979. *Multinomial Probit*. New York: Academic Press.

Debreu, G., 1960. 'Review of R. D. Luce's *Individual Choice Behavior,' American Economic Review* **50,** 186–8.

Domencich, T. A. and D. McFadden, 1975. *Urban Travel Demand: A Behavioral Analysis*. Amsterdam: North Holland.

Farrell, M. J. 1954. 'The demand for motorcars in the United States,' *Journal of the Royal Statistical Society,* A **117,** 171–200.

Fechner, G. T., 1860. *Elemente der Psychophysik*. Leipzig: Breitkopf und Hartel.

Finney, D., 1971. *Probit Analysis*. Cambridge: Cambridge University Press.

Fisher, R. A. and F. Yates, 1957. *Statistical Tables for Biological, Agricultural and Medical Research* (3rd edn). Edinburgh: Oliver and Boyd.

Fomby, T. B., R. C. Hill and S. R. Johnson, 1984. *Advanced Econometric Methods*. New York: Springer.
Gaddum, J. H., 1933. *Reports on Biological Standard III. Methods of Biological Assay Depending on a Quantal Response*. Special Report Series of the Medical Research Council, no. 183. London: Medical Research Council.
Goldberger, A. S., 1964. *Econometric Theory*. New York: Wiley.
Hausman, J. and D. McFadden, 1984. 'Specification tests for the multinomial logit model,' *Econometrica* **52,** 1219–40.
Hausman, J. A. and D. A. Wise, 1978. 'A conditional probit model for qualitative discrete decisions recognizing interdependence and heterogeneous preferences,' *Econometrica* **46,** 403–26.
Johnson, N. L., and S. Kotz, 1970. *Distributions in Statistics: Continuous Univariate Distributions* (2 vols). New York: Wiley.
Johnston, J., 1984. *Econometric Methods* (3rd edn). Auckland: McGraw-Hill.
Judge, G. G., W. E. Griffiths, R. C. Hill and T. C. Lee, 1980. *The Theory and Practice of Econometrics*. New York: Wiley.
Kay, R. and S. Little, 1986. 'Assessing the fit of the logistic model: a case study of children with the Haemolytic Uraemic syndrome,' *Applied Statistics,* **35,** 16–30.
Ladd, G. W., 1966. 'Linear probability functions and discriminant functions,' *Econometrica* **34,** 873–85.
Lancaster, K. L., 1971. *Consumer Demand: A New Approach*. New York: Columbia University Press.
Lancaster, T., 1979. 'Prediction from binary choice models—a note,' *Journal of Econometrics* **9,** 387–90.
Lerman, S. R. and M. Ben-Akiva, 1976. 'Disaggregate behavioral model of automobile ownership,' *Transportation Research Record* **569,** 34–55.
Luce, R., 1959. *Individual Choice Behavior*. New York: Wiley.
Luce, R., and P. Suppes, 1965. 'Preferences, utility, and subjective probability,' in R. Luce, R. Bush and E. Galanter (eds) *Handbook of Mathematical Psychology*. New York: Wiley.
McCullagh, P. and J. A. Nelder, 1983. *Generalized Linear Models*. London: Chapman and Hall.
McFadden, D., 1974. 'Conditional logit analysis of qualitative choice behavior,' in P. Zarembka (ed), *Frontiers in Econometrics*. New York: Academic Press.
McFadden, D. and F. Reid, 1975. 'Aggregate travel demand forecasting from disaggregated behavioral models,' *Transportation Research Record,* **534,** pp. 24–37.
McFadden, D., 1976. 'Quantal choice analysis: a survey,' *Annals of Economic and Social Measurement* **5,** 363–90.
McFadden, D., 1977. 'Econometric models of probabilistic choice,' in C. F. Manski and D. McFadden (eds), *Structural Analysis of Discrete Data with Econometric Applications,* Cambridge, Mass.: MIT Press.
Maddala, G. S., 1983. *Limited-dependent and Qualitative Variables in Econometrics*. Cambridge: Cambridge University Press.
Manski, C. F., 1977. 'The structure of random utility models,' *Theory and Decision* **8,** 229–54.
Manski, C. F. and S. Lerman, 1977. 'The estimation of choice probabilities from choice based samples,' *Econometrica* **45,** 1977–88.
Manski, C. F. and D. McFadden (eds), 1977a. *Structural Analysis of Discrete Data with Econometric Applications*. Cambridge, Mass.: MIT Press.
Manski, C. F. and D. McFadden, 1977b. 'Alternative estimators and sample design for discrete choice,' in C. F. Manski and D. McFadden (eds) *Structural Analysis of Discrete Data with Econometric Applications*. Cambridge, Mass.: MIT Press.

Meadows, D. H., D. L. Meadows, J. Randers and W. W. Behrens, 1972. *The Limits to Growth.* New York: Universe Books.

Miner, J. R., 1933. 'Pierre-François Verhulst, the discoverer of the logistic curve,' *Human Biology* **5,** 673–89.

Mood, A. M., F. A. Graybill and D. C. Boes, 1974. *Introduction to the Theory of Statistics* (3rd edn). New York: McGraw-Hill.

Mot, E. S., J. S. Cramer and E. M. van der Gulik, 1989. *De Keuze van een Betaalmiddel.* Amsterdam: Stichting voor Economisch Onderzoek.

Orcutt, G. H., M. Greenberger, J. Korbel and A. M. Rivlin, 1961. *Microanalysis of Socio-economic Systems.* New York: Harper.

Pearl, R., 1927. 'The indigenous population of Algeria in 1926,' *Science* **66,** 593–4.

Pearl, R. and L. J. Reed, 1920. 'On the rate of growth of the population of the United States since 1970 and its mathematical representation,' *Proceedings of the National Academy of Sciences* **6,** 275–88.

Pearl, R., C. P. Winsor and F. B. White, 1928. 'The form of the growth curve of the cantaloupe (Cucumis melo) under field conditions,' *Proceedings of the National Academy of Sciences* **14,** 895–901.

Pearl, R., L. J. Reed and J. F. Kish, 1940. 'The logistic curve and the census count of 1940,' *Science* **92,** 486–8.

Pregibon, D., 1981. 'Logistic regression diagnostics,' *The Annals of Statistics,* **9,** 705–24.

Rao, C. R., 1955. 'Theory of the method of estimation by minimum chi-square,' *Bulletin de l'Institut International de Statistique* **35,** 25–32.

Reed, L. J. and J. Berkson, 1929. 'The application of the logistic function to experimental data,' *Journal of Physical Chemistry* **33,** 760–79.

Ross, S. M., 1977. *Introduction to Probability Models.* New York: Harcourt Brace Jovanovich.

Steckel, J. H. and W. R. Vanhonacker, 1988. 'A heterogeneous conditional logit model of choice,' *Journal of Business and Economic Statistics* **6,** 391–8.

Theil, H., 1969. 'A multinomial extension of the linear logit model,' *International Economic Review* **10,** 251–9.

Thurstone, L., 1927. 'A law of comparative judgment,' *Psychological Review* **34,** 273–86.

Westin, R. B., 1974. 'Predictions from binary choice models,' *Journal of Econometrics* **2,** 1–16.

Winsor, C. P., 1932. 'A comparison of certain symmetrical growth curves,' *Journal of the Washington Academy of Sciences* **22,** 73–84.

Author Index

Subject Index